West African Studies

Urbanisation Dynamics in West Africa 1950–2010

AFRICAPOLIS I, 2015 UPDATE

François Moriconi-Ebrard, Dominique Harre
and Philipp Heinrigs

Please cite this publication as:
Moriconi-Ebrard, F., D. Harre and P. Heinrigs (2016), *Urbanisation Dynamics in West Africa 1950-2010: Africapolis I, 2015 Update,* West African Studies, OECD Publishing, Paris.
http://dx.doi.org/10.1787/9789264252233-en

ISBN 978-92-64-25222-6 (print)
ISBN 978-92-64-25223-3 (PDF)

Series: West African Studies
ISSN 2074-3548 (print)
ISSN 2074-353X (online)

Photo credits: Cover © Philippe Krueger/BUREAU.PK, Berlin.

Revised version, March 2016.
Details of revisions available at: *www.oecd.org/about/publishing/Corrigendum-UrbanisationDynamicsWestAfrica.pdf.*

Corrigenda to OECD publications may be found on line at: *www.oecd.org/about/publishing/corrigenda.htm.*

Foreword

For more than two decades, the Sahel and West Africa Club has highlighted the importance of settlement dynamics and in particular its most spectacular manifestation, urbanisation, in order to understand the important role it plays in the economic, social and political transformations in the region. The publication of the *West African Long-Term Perspectives Study* in 1998 was a major contribution towards understanding and anticipating the impact of settlement dynamics in West Africa. More recently, the Club highlighted the central role cities and urban-rural linkages play in agricultural transformation and growth, agro-food value chain development and food security (*Settlement, Market and Food Security*).

Cities and their inhabitants are increasingly at the heart of development processes in African countries. However, there is still little data on the actual size of West African cities, their number, location, the distances between them, where and how they form and grow. Yet this information is increasingly important in informing a wide range of development policies at the local, national and regional level, such as urban and land planning, public service provision, infrastructure and investment, decentralisation and spatial development, as well as energy and climate change.

To further develop our multidisciplinary work and to provide a reliable, comparable and homogenous database (available at **stats.oecd.org**), the Sahel and West Africa Club Secretariat funded the update of the Africapolis I database which is part of the e-Geopolis programme. e-Geopolis applies a methodology combining satellite imagery and census data to identify, localise and estimate the physical and demographic size of African cities. The 2015 update provides important improvements to data coverage and our understanding of the state of urbanisation and urbanisation dynamics in West Africa. It integrates new census data for 13 countries and more recent high definition aerial images. Although statistical data weaknesses persist, this is undoubtedly the best available picture yet of contemporary urbanisation in West Africa for the period 1950 to 2010.

Africapolis was originally financed in 2008 by the Agence française de développement (AFD) with support from the French National Research Agency (ANR).

Acknowledgements: The publication was written by François Moriconi-Ebrard (CNRS, e-Geopolis), Dominique Harre (e-Geopolis) and Philipp Heinrigs (Sahel and West Africa Club Secretariat/OECD). Editorial guidance was provided by Marie Trémolières (SWAC/OECD Secretariat) and contributions to the text were made by Thomas Allen (SWAC/OECD Secretariat). The SWAC Secretariat team would like to especially thank Lia Beyeler (SWAC/OECD Secretariat), Cathy Chatel (e-Geopolis), Eric Denis (CNRS, e-Geopolis), Sylvie Letassey (SWAC/OECD Secretariat) and Rafael Prieto Curiel (University College London).

The Sahel and West Africa Club

Working together for regional integration

The Sahel and West Africa Club (SWAC) is an international platform for policy dialogue and analysis devoted to regional issues in West Africa. Its mission is to enhance the effectiveness of regional action in the common and interdependent area composed of the 17 countries of ECOWAS, UEMOA and CILSS. Created in 1976, it is the only international entity entirely dedicated to regional co-operation in Africa.

Some 100 stakeholders participate in the SWAC platform: governments of West African countries and OECD member countries, regional organisations, professional associations and civil society groups, bi- and multi-lateral development partners and research centres.

Under the guidance of its Members, the Secretariat of the SWAC provides factual, innovative and forward-looking analysis; facilitates dialogue, information-sharing and consensus-building; and formulates policy recommendations. Based at the OECD, the Secretariat helps ensure West Africa's presence in global fora.

Members

Austria: Federal Ministry for Europe, Integration and Foreign Affairs -Austrian Development Cooperation (ADA); **Belgium:** Ministry of Foreign Affairs, Foreign Trade and Development Cooperation; **CILSS:** Executive Secretariat of the Permanent Interstates Committee for Drought Control in the Sahel ; **ECOWAS:** Commission of the Economic Community of West African States; **France:** Ministry of Foreign Affairs and International Development; **Luxembourg:** Ministry of Foreign and European Affairs; **Netherlands:** Ministry of Foreign Affairs; **Switzerland:** Federal Department of Foreign Affairs- Swiss Agency for Development and Cooperation (SDC); **UEMOA:** Commission of the West African Economic and Monetary Union; **United States:** U.S. Agency for International Development (USAID)

The European Union is an important partner and contributes to the financing of the SWAC programme of work, in particular activities linked to food security and resilience.

As Observers, the African Union and the NEPAD Planning and Coordinating Agency, the Canadian Ministry of Foreign Affairs, Trade and Development, and the Network of Farmers' Organisations and Agricultural Producers of West Africa (ROPPA) are closely associated with SWAC activities.

For more information:
www.oecd.org/swac
http://stats.oecd.org

Contact:
E-mail swac.contact@oecd.org

The global e-Geopolis programme

Localise, measure and standardise data

The e-Geopolis programme, financed by the French National Research Agency (ANR), seeks to provide a comparable and comprehensive measurement of worldwide urbanisation, applicable on many geographic levels, from local to international. Comparative regional analysis and cross-country comparisons of urbanisation dynamics require homogeneous, standardised data, yet urbanisation data is based on diverse national definitions. The e-Geopolis programme aims to fill this gap. Africapolis is the regional programme of e-Geopolis focusing on Africa. Financed by the French Development Agency (AFD), the Africapolis programme began in 2008 with three phases: Africapolis I (West Africa, 2008), Africapolis II (East and Central Africa, 2011), and Africapolis III (Southern Africa).

A unique method recognised by the international scientific community

To best deal with measurement issues, e-Geopolis uses a standard definition of "urban" and a methodology correlating satellite images and general population census data published by national statistical institutions. e-Geopolis also provides precise geo-references for each unit, allowing cross-referencing of morphological information with qualitative and quantitative information. The ensuing data is comparable, independent of national definitions and verifiable.

Comparable

States differ in size, shape and configuration. National borders divide population groups, natural environments and areas that were initially homogeneous. However, "cities" have been defined at the national level, impeding cross-national comparisons. Thus, by applying one sole definition, e-Geopolis provides the possibility to map, understand and measure the dynamics throughout West Africa and compare the results to other regions on the continent and globally.

Independent of national definitions

The definition of "urban" is not without strategic importance and can influence how states interpret the data. By modifying population thresholds and functional constraints (i.e., whether an urban area must be an administrative centre or not) and by dividing an urban area into several independent communities, completely different configurations of urban systems, pictures of rural/urban migration, and urban hierarchies, for example, can appear. The e-Geopolis definition, a minimum of 10 000 inhabitants in a continuously built-up area with less than 200 metres between buildings, is applied no matter the national definition.

Verifiable

The two criteria of the e-Geopolis definition of urban are verifiable. The demographic data used is from official and public sources and, unless otherwise indicated, from population and housing censuses. The expansion of built up areas is observable on the ground, comparable to maps and can be super-imposed with satellite images through Google Earth.

Table of contents

Boxes

Figures

Maps

Plates

Tables

Executive summary

In 1950, West Africa counted 152 urban agglomerations with more than 10 000 inhabitants. In 2010, the region numbered 1 947 urban agglomerations, including sub-Saharan Africa's largest city Lagos with 10.6 million inhabitants. These towns and cities are home to 133 million people or 41% of West Africa's total population. The large majority of these people live in a town that did not exist in 1950 or which was only a small village. Cities and their inhabitants are increasingly shaping the region's economic, political and social landscape. Yet there is little up-to-date data available allowing for a better understanding of the urbanisation dynamics that are profoundly reshaping the region.

This information is essential for implementing a wide range of development policies at the local, national and regional level. These include urban and land planning, public service provision, infrastructure and investment strategies, as well as decentralisation and spatial development policies. The fact that a country's population increases, or that its level of urbanisation doubles, does not necessarily provide any information on the spatial redistribution that accompanies these population dynamics, such as the geographic distribution of towns, their size, their number, or the distance between them. Researchers, governments and development partners need this information to analyse their impact, to design national policies and to plan for future trends.

The Africapolis I project was a major contribution to improving geo-statistical knowledge of urbanisation dynamics in West Africa. The applied method combines the use of demographic sources[1], satellite and aerial imagery and other cartographic sources to provide population estimates at the level of an individual agglomeration. The availability of disaggregated data allows for the integration of spatial structures in urban development and territorial transformation analyses. Furthermore, Africapolis data is harmonised, applying a homogenous definition of urban, irrespective of national definitions, and can be used for cross-country and regional analysis.

This update of the 2008 Africapolis I[2] study provides population estimates for 2010 of 2 965 identified agglomerations in West Africa, of which 1 947 have more than 10 000 inhabitants. In addition, this study provides four types of new information:

1. a systematic geolocation of urban agglomerations;
2. the identification of "small cities" ranging from 10 000 to 100 000 inhabitants;
3. a description of territorial transformations resulting from morphological processes;
4. an inventory of 1 236 agglomerations in Nigeria.

The identification of cities with fewer than 100 000 inhabitants is a major contribution of the Africapolis programme. Most databases, including that of the United Nations, only list cities of more than 100 000 inhabitants. Yet in 2010, 90% of West Africa's cities had fewer than 100 000 inhabitants. This represents a combined population of 45 million people. Moreover, new urban agglomerations continue to emerge at the bottom of the urban hierarchy, with 565 new urban agglomerations since 2000.

The study highlights the importance of small- and medium-sized agglomerations in national urban networks and the emergence of new urban agglomerations through *in situ* urbanisation, a key characteristic in West Africa. The proliferation of small towns, whose urban attributes are debatable, is explained by a confluence of factors in each national context. These include the combination of decentralisation policies, pre-colonial legacies (e.g. Nigeria) and colonial legacies (coastal capitals and spatial redistribution). Also, strong demographic growth over past decades has been an important factor. The number of small agglomerations further emphasises the relative weakness of secondary cities in national urban hierarchies and thereby increases the weight of metropolises.

The morphological approach adopted by Africapolis helps identify territorial transformation processes in West Africa, which remain little explained and poorly measured with the exception of a few metropolises.[3] The morphological processes induced by strong urban growth are at the core of better understanding complex urbanisation dynamics and can be observed at several levels: metropolises, secondary cities, merging of villages and the formation of conurbations.[4] These processes are:

- the strong sprawl of metropolitan regions, such as Nouakchott, Ouagadougou, Conakry and Freetown;
- the strong irregular sprawl of numerous secondary cities, following a model similar to metropolises;
- significant merging processes at various levels in countries or regions with high population densities, for example in Benin and Ghana where urban agglomerations emerge from the merging of villages;
- the formation of meta-urban conurbations, in particular in Nigeria.

The territorial development processes underway share a common key characteristic: habitat densification coupled with demographic pressure leads to "scattered urbanisation" of areas officially considered rural. The conurbations and agglomerations created as a result of the merging of villages, are pushing the frontier of what is urban. The criteria that distinguish urban from rural are being re-examined one by one (ex. densities, type of housing and the importance of agriculture) and are changing the understanding of urbanisation in West African countries. In Nigeria in particular, the transition from hyper-rural to meta-urban is disrupting the hierarchy of the national urban network. For example, Onitsha, Nigeria, became the country's second largest agglomeration with 6.28 million inhabitants after merging with twenty agglomerations over the past 20 years.

The new measurement of urbanisation dynamics in Nigeria constitutes probably the most complete data on urbanisation dynamics in this country. 1 236 agglomerations have been identified (compared to 607 in the 2008 study) of which 1 020 had more than 10 000 inhabitants in 2010. The new data has detected the emergence of large conurbations in the dense Niger Delta region and a significant increase in the number of small agglomerations, two phenomena not sufficiently recognised in the 2008 edition.

The 2015 update of Africapolis I significantly improves our geo-statistical knowledge and understanding of West African urbanisation dynamics. The new data compiled is broader and more reliable. However, the statistical situation remains problematic, particularly in Nigeria. Data inconsistencies and geographic and historical gaps in census coverage, remain a major constraint in analysing urbanisation dynamics in the region.

NOTES

1 *In most cases these are from general population and housing censuses and official headcounts published by national statistical institutes.*

2 *Africapolis I was published in 2008 and estimated the population of urban agglomerations in 2000 and provided projections for 2010 and 2020. The number of identified agglomerations was 1 582.*

3 *The State of African Cities 2010, United Nations Human Settlements Programme (UN-HABITAT).*

4 *A conurbation is defined here as one continuous agglomeration formed by the merging of at least two initially distinct urban agglomerations.*

Updating knowledge on urbanisation in West Africa

Within Africa, the least urbanised continent in the world, West African urbanisation reached 41% in 2010. National variations range from 18% in Niger to 48% in Côte d'Ivoire and The Gambia. An urban transition is very much underway, especially in Nigeria with its long history of urbanisation. The analysis of quantitative data and indicators highlights recent and emerging urbanisation dynamics that must be taken into account in the formulation of development, investment and infrastructure policies.

This study updates data and results of two preceding e-Geopolis analyses: Africapolis I (2008), studying the urbanisation of 16 West African countries; and, Africapolis II (2011), studying 19 East and Central African countries. Covered in Africapolis II, Chad, a country of 1.3 million km^2 and 20 million inhabitants in 2010, is included in this work. However, this study goes beyond a simple data update by integrating newly available national population censuses, more complete geolocation information of settlement areas, and a more widespread use of the most recent (post–2008) high resolution satellite images. It provides a comprehensive overview of agglomerations of 10 000 or more inhabitants between 1950 and 2010 for the 17 countries covered: Benin, Burkina Faso, Cape Verde, Chad, Côte d'Ivoire, The Gambia, Ghana, Guinea, Guinea-Bissau, Liberia, Mali, Mauritania, Niger, Nigeria, Senegal, Sierra Leone and Togo.

THE NEW FEATURES OF THE UPDATE

The following three categories of data were used to identify and measure urban agglomerations and have been updated since Africapolis I. In addition, specific work was carried out on Nigeria.

Integration of new census data

For 13 countries (Benin, Burkina Faso, Cape Verde, Chad, Ghana, Guinea-Bissau, Liberia, Mali, Mauritania, Niger, Nigeria, Senegal and Togo) new census data became available (Table 1.2) and contributed to an in-depth re-evaluation of population figures in 2010.

Systematic updating of urban surface areas

The availability of more recent (from 2007 to 2012) and higher resolution images than in 2008 helped revise urban surface areas, i.e. their morphological shape. The urban surface area is the built-up area of an agglomeration and depicted as a polygon. The review led to a reassessment of the size of numerous agglomerations, identification of recent processes of coalescence or absorption of urban areas previously considered distinct (Benin, Guinea-Bissau, Mali and Nigeria) and to a more accurate measurement of the size of small agglomerations (from 10 000 to 50 000 inhabitants). This information refines the examination of the morphological processes underway that underpin the emergence of new urban forms.

Precise geolocation of "local units"

"Local units" represent the administrative base unit, whether villages or towns, for counting the population. Up until the 21st century, local units were not geo-localised but placed within a superior hierarchical administrative division (canton, department, etc.). The updating helped integrate accurate geographic coordinates of several tens of thousands of local units, in particular in Cape Verde, Côte d'Ivoire, Guinea, Mali, Senegal, as well as large parts of Niger and The Gambia. All the villages in Burkina Faso and Benin were already geo-localised in the 2008 study.

A comprehensive analysis of Nigeria

Identifying agglomerations and an estimation of Nigeria's population based on 2006 census data, although still incomplete, provides probably the only detailed measure of urbanisation existing today in this country. Nigeria, accounting for more than half of West Africa's urban population, presents a considerable challenge. Identifying agglomerations implies a systematic scanning of the country's surface area, more than 900 000 km². 1 236 agglomerations have thus been identified (compared to 607 in the 2008 study) of which 1 020 had more than 10 000 inhabitants in 2010. This work also helped identify the emergence of large conurbations in the dense Niger Delta region.

Figure 0.1
Number of identified agglomerations Africapolis I 2008 vs. Africapolis I – 2015 update

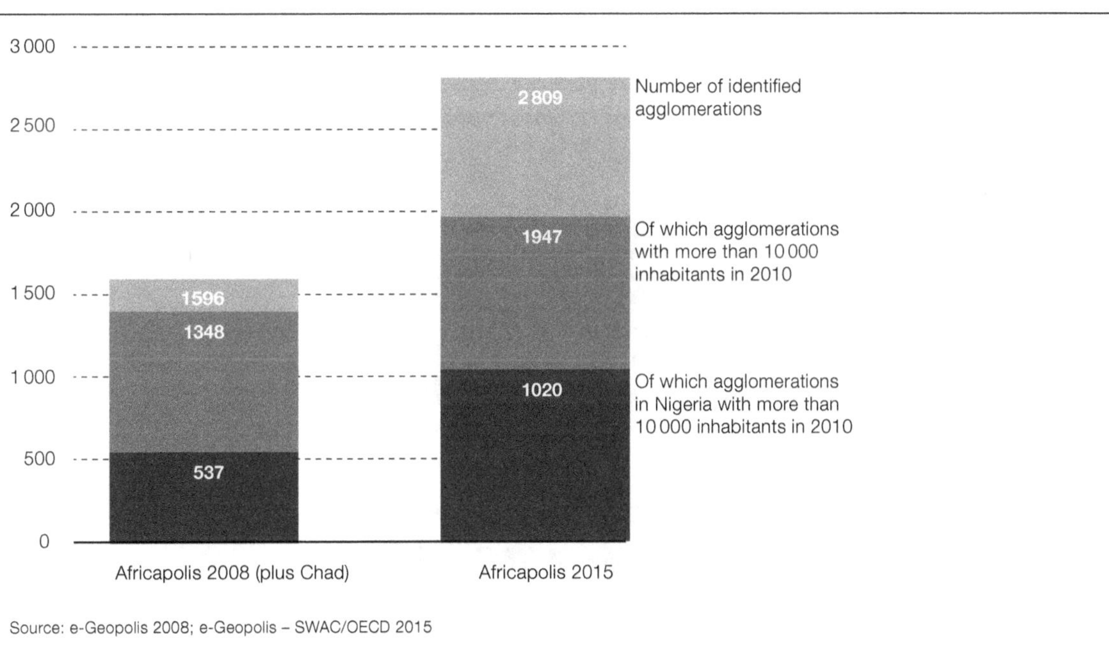

Source: e-Geopolis 2008; e-Geopolis – SWAC/OECD 2015

Projecting the number of new urban agglomerations appearing by 2030

In 1950, there were only 152 urban agglomerations in West Africa. Since then, the number of agglomerations has increased 13-fold, reaching 1 947. In 2010, 43% of the region's urban population lived in an agglomeration that did not exist in 1950 or which was only a small village. One of the challenges in projecting the urban population is to be able to estimate the share of new cities in the sample of urban agglomerations. Herein lies the difficulty and the specificity of this exercise compared to classic demographic projections, which provide data by country or by local administrative divisions whose number does not change.

To allow for a projection of the number of agglomerations that will exceed 10 000 inhabitants in 2020 and in 2030[1], agglomerations are being inventoried once they exceed 5 000 inhabitants. Taking into account the United Nations' projection for slowing population growth, it is projected that 99% of the agglomerations which currently number between 5 000 and 9 999 inhabitants will exceed 10 000 inhabitants in 2030. New agglomerations, with less than 5 000 inhabitants or which did not exist in 2010, will probably increase these figures.

Update of the physical expansion of agglomerations since 2008

The urban surface areas were reviewed based on recent high resolution images, dated 2008–12 (Plate 0.1). No new images were available for southern Cote d'Ivoire, central Ghana and Liberia. All agglomerations with 50 000 or more inhabitants are documented by recent and high quality images, though the images of large urban centres are in many cases not from the same dates due to their larger geographic expansion.

Plate 0.1
Expansion of the urban area: Example of Bobo Dioulasso, Burkina Faso, 2003–12

Sources: Google Earth (2012), Bobo Dioulasso, Burkina Faso,
Available at http://www.google.com/earth/download/ge/agree.html (Viewed 29 November 2012)

Notes: Yellow line - outline of agglomeration as used in 2008; red line – outline of agglomeration as used in this study

Box 0.1

Comparison with Africapolis I 2008

The general results of the 2015 update are compared with those of 2008 by taking into account: the size of the urban population, the level of urbanisation, the number of agglomerations, the size of metropolises and the primacy indices (Table 0.1).

Nigeria, Mali and Chad show significant differences compared to the 2008 study:

- In Nigeria, the level of urbanisation is re-assessed at 46%, up from 31%, linked to the increase in the number of urban agglomerations, and to the identification of large conurbations in the Niger River Delta. The identification of the Onitsha conurbation, the second largest agglomeration in Nigeria and which does not appear on the list of the ten biggest agglomerations in the country in the 2008 study, is the most spectacular example.

- In Mali, a better appreciation of Bamako's size (+46%) and the identification of new agglomerations (as a result of newly available population data by village), explains the revision of the level of urbanisation from 22% to 30%. The newly identified agglomerations are mostly small agglomerations of 10 000 to 50 000 inhabitants created by the expansion of villages and which are officially categorised as rural. The re-evaluation of Bamako's size is explained by the identification and counting of suburbs during the 2009 census. These areas are still officially considered "villages" although six of them numbered over 15 000 inhabitants in 2010, including Kalabancoro (132 000 inhabitants) and Dialakorodji (close to 50 000).

- In Chad, taking into account the 2009 census results led to a readjustment of the size of agglomerations and the identification of new ones. In addition, 15 refugee camps are included in the list.

The countries where urbanisation dynamics have been revised downwards are Liberia (from 50% to 44%), Benin (45% to 40%) and Cape Verde (50% to 47%). In Benin, the decline is due to the use of a new adjusted local administrative divisions, unavailable in 2008[1]. In Cape Verde and Liberia, the data from new censuses have been integrated (2010 and 2008, respectively). As a result,and strongly influenced by Nigeria, the regional level of urbanisation is evaluated up from 33% to 41%.

NOTE

1 *The population is now evaluated by the aggregation of "villages" and "neighbourhoods" and is no longer estimated on the basis of a district's population.*

Table 0.1
Africapolis I 2008 and the 2015 update (for 2010)

	Urban population (millions)		Level of urbanisation (in %)		Number of urban agglomerations		Size of metropole(s) (millions)		Primacy index	
	AP I 2008	2015 update	AP I 2008	2015 update	AP I 2008	2015 update	AP I 2008	2015 update	AP I 2008	2015 update
Benin	4.02	3.58	45	40	83	81	1.26	1.16	4.0	2.4
Burkina Faso	3.89	4.34	26	26	87	82	1.38	1.91	2.9	3.4
Cabo Verde	0.26	0.23	50	47	6	4	0.13	0.13	1.6	1.9
Chad	2.39	3.02	20	26	42	75	1.04	1.01	7.7	7.0
Côte d'Ivoire	9.52	9.46	45	48	157	166	4.11	3.97	6.7	6.7
Gambia	0.75	0.84	45	48	7	10	0.58	0.60	8.1	7.2
Ghana	9.97	10.93	44	45	151	173	3.45	3.63	1.9	1.6
Guinea	3.02	3.19	34	32	26	39	1.58	1.41	8.7	8.5
Guinea-Bissau	0.56	0.60	37	38	8	6	0.46	0.46	18.7	7.5
Liberia	1.64	1.61	50	44	18	23	1.26	1.17	24.5	25.7
Mali	2.94	4.59	22	30	45	71	1.55	2.27	9.7	9.4
Mauritania	0.97	1.13	31	35	11	16	0.70	0.74	8.4	8.5
Niger	2.33	2.81	18	18	46	51	0.87	1.17	4.2	5.6
Nigeria	48.48	76.42	31	46	509	1 020	15.41	16.87	3.2	1.7
Senegal	5.42	5.58	45	46	53	57	2.75	2.56	5.2	3.7
Sierra Leone	1.44	1.67	26	28	14	19	0.89	0.93	5.5	5.5
Togo	2.78	2.79	47	46	57	54	1.41	1.45	12.0	11.0
West Africa	100.38	132.79	33	41	1 320	1 947				

* In the 2008 Africapolis I study, figures for 2010 were projections based on 2000 estimates.

Source: Africapolis I, 2008; Africapolis II, 2009; e-Geopolis – SWAC/OECD 2015

Confirmation of the trends identified in 2008

The results did not yield any major surprises but rather refined earlier results and further improved the data's reliability. The report does not challenge the global indicators by country, nor the major trends, which have simply accentuated. Besides Nigeria, the update revealed an increase in the estimated and projected number of agglomerations for 2010 and, in some cases, their size (e.g. Bamako, Ouagadougou).

The results also confirm the advantages of using a morphological approach to identify the most active urbanisation dynamics and to take these into account when planning rural and urban land policies as well as urban and transport governance programmes. Thus, the spatial expansion of some capitals (Conakry, Freetown, Nouakchott, Ouagadougou) and numerous secondary agglomerations follows a model similar to metropolises, with significant merging processes at various levels. Measuring these processes illustrates that the large conurbations[2] emerging from these processes are changing the understanding of urbanisation in West African countries.

NOTES

1 *The work on projections is not included in this report.*

2 *A conurbation is defined here as one continuous agglomeration, formed by the merging of at least two former urban agglomerations.*

Bibliography

AFD (2010), "Africapolis II – Dynamiques urbaines en Afrique centrale et orientale, 1950–2020", and Fiches pays 2011, Agence Française de Développement, Paris, http://e-geopolis.eu/IMG/pdf/AFRICAPOLIS_II_resume.pdf.

AFD (2008), "Africapolis I – Dynamiques de l'urbanisation, 1950–2020: Approche géo-statistique, Afrique de l'Ouest", Agence Française de Développement, Paris, http://www.afd.fr/webdav/shared/PUBLICATIONS/THEMATIQUES/autres-publications/BT/Africapolis_Rapport.pdf.

Cour, J. and S. Snrech (eds.) (1998), *Preparing for the Future - A Vision of West Africa in the Year 2020*, West Africa Long-Term Perspective Study (WALTPS), OECD Publishing, Paris, http://dx.doi.org/10.1787/9789264174320-en.

OECD (2013), *Settlement, Market and Food Security*, West African Studies, OECD Publishing, Paris, http://dx.doi.org/10.1787/9789264187443-en.

Chapter 1

Challenges in tracking change in West African settlement dynamics

1.1 THE DEFINITION OF URBAN

Measuring the size of the urban population, the level of urbanisation or the number of urban agglomerations depends on the chosen definition of urban. Definitions in West Africa, like elsewhere, vary from country to country. The definition of urban varies from 1 500 (Guinea Bissau) to 20 000 inhabitants (Nigeria) if a numerical threshold is used, but in some cases administrative status is used to determine what is considered urban (e.g. Chad). To allow for regional and international comparisons, only one definition of urban is used for all countries. The definition of urban agglomerations is based on two criteria, the land use and the quantity of the population:

1. An agglomeration is a continuously built-up and developed area, with less than 200 metres between two buildings.
2. An agglomeration is considered urban if it has a minimum of 10 000 agglomerated inhabitants.

The interpretation of the label "urban" can differ according to viewpoint (social, economic, political, anthropological, etc.). Similarly, it can contradict national classifications that consider agglomerations that have 10 000 inhabitants or more as rural, or do not even consider them as agglomerations. In the opposite case, there are agglomerations with less than 10 000 inhabitants that warrant a designation as "urban". Using one single numerical definition allows for defining the same object irrespective of environment, country or region where it is located.

The compilation of urban data is based on the detection of built-up zones (urban areas) from high-resolution satellite imagery. The largest agglomerations (greater than 1 km^2) are then identified based on directories of districts or villages published as part of population censuses. The number of inhabitants is then estimated as the sum of the inhabitants of the local units comprised by the agglomeration[1].

There are two cases:

1. An urban agglomeration is within the perimetre of one local unit. The agglomeration's urban population then corresponds to the population of the local unit.
2. An urban agglomeration expands over several local units. In this case, the agglomeration takes on the name of the local unit that ranks highest in the hierarchy. If they are at the same hierarchical level, it is the most populated local unit that takes precedence. This local unit would be considered de facto as the "centre"; the others would be the "outskirts".

1.2 THE GEOLOCATION OF LOCAL UNITS: MAJOR ADVANCES

Censuses do not locate local units. The geolocation of local units, i.e. the assigning of terrestrial geographic coordinates, is a major step in building the database. Assigning local units geographic coordinates allows for cross-referencing with identified morphological information and with local units' qualitative and quantitative information (classifying aspects, population data).

In Africa, the geolocation of local units is one of the biggest obstacles in studying population and settlement dynamics. In 2008, only 2 500 local units had been identified. Today, close to 200 000 local units distributed over

Table 1.1

Local units by country

	Number (rounded)	Population data	Geolocalisation	Cross-referencing population/geolocalisation
Benin	3 000	yes	yes	yes
Burkina Faso	7 600	yes	yes	yes
Cabo Verde	400	yes	yes	yes
Chad	22 500	yes	yes	no
Côte d'Ivoire	8 500	yes	yes	yes
Gambia	1 000	yes	yes	possible
Ghana	60 000	yes	Non	no
Guinea	16 000	yes	yes	no
Guinea-Bissau	1 000	no	yes	no
Liberia	3 500	incoherent	yes	no
Mali	13 000	yes	yes	yes
Mauritania	5 500	yes	yes	possible
Niger	11 000	yes	non-exhaustive	partial
Nigeria	24 000	no	partial	no
Senegal	13 500	yes	yes	no
Sierra Leone	5 000	no	partial	possible
Togo	4 000	yes	non-exhaustive	partial
TOTAL	199 500			

Source: e-Geopolis – SWAC/OECD 2015

an area of 7.4 million km^2 have been identified (Table 1.1). However, some uncertainties persist:

- The number of local units, even rounded, is constantly changing. For example, in Mauritania, the number of identified "inhabited areas" more than doubled between 1977 and 2000, from 2 342 to 5 551.
- The definition of local units varies from country to country. In Ghana "settlements" are inhabited areas, whereas in Côte d'Ivoire villages and municipalities are territorial constituencies. Besides the main village, these constituencies can include several dozen settlements that are not geolocated. In Senegal, like in Côte d'Ivoire, there are two levels of villages, the "village-centre" and the "big village", which includes hamlets and isolated farms, that are however named and geo-referenced.
- No official directories for Nigeria or Sierra Leone have been found. Guinea-Bissau has not published national population and housing census results by local unit. In Liberia two contradicting lists exist.
- The geolocation of local units has never been carried out in Ghana, and only partially in Niger.
- Inconsistencies when cross-checking two sources from different institutions: one, the population census, and the other, the

geolocation through a ministry (agriculture, defence, geographical services). The lists of local units of various ministries, sometimes within the same service, do not match and dates may vary.

Information on local units remains difficult to obtain, whether it be population numbers or geographic coordinates. Nevertheless, the quality of the information continues to improve.

Method applied to update population data

Population statistics not only provide information on the size of urban population, but are also used to estimate the total population, from which indicators such as the level of urbanisation can be calculated.

The Africapolis database provides population estimates for harmonised dates (1 July 1950, 1960, 1970, 1980, 1990, 2000, 2010). Unless otherwise indicated, population data is calculated based on census and counting results carried out between 1948 and 2012. There is little reliable state-provided data in this region. Estimations by national statistical institutes are usually simple projections. The numbers are lined up by geometric interpolation, or if there is no source, by retropolating past dates and projecting future dates. 2010 data for Guinea and Côte d'Ivoire are projections due to the lack of recent sources (Table 1.2).

The Africapolis I 2015 update database integrates new data from population censuses published since 2008. Some censuses are earlier than 2008 (Burkina Faso, Senegal, Nigeria) but were not available in 2008. In total, 13 countries are concerned: Benin, Burkina Faso, Cape Verde, Chad, Ghana, Guinea-Bissau, Liberia, Mali, Mauritania, Niger, Nigeria, Senegal and Togo.

1.3 THE SPECIAL CASE OF NIGERIA

A different method was used for Nigeria. Due to the lack of reliable population statistics, it was not possible to estimate the population of agglomerations by cross-checking population with morphological data. The approach is described in detail in Chapter 4. Initially developed by Denis in 2008 for Africapolis I, it is further improved in terms of the analysis of data sources and the use of global models to estimate the population of urban agglomerations. On the one hand, this approach integrates features of local settlement patterns by relying on the systematic mapping of agglomerations and their physical imprint; and, on the other hand, by relying on theoretical models that characterise settlement systems.

1.4 PERSISTENT PROBLEMS, BUT A MINE OF NEW INFORMATION

Even though there has been a significant improvement in the understanding of West African settlement dynamics, there are still many technical constraints: geographic and historic gaps in census coverage, massive population movement, lack of accuracy of some publications, difficulty in locating villages and ambiguity in toponyms of towns. Hence, the data provided still presents a certain degree of uncertainty.

Knowledge has increased despite these methodological obstacles. For instance, this method enables the estimation of new agglomerations exceeding 10 000 between 2010 and 2030. These emerging agglomerations, dispersed throughout the territory, will contribute to territorial linking, with the average distance between urban agglomerations constantly shrinking. With the number of agglomerations increasing within a defined geographic space, towns are moving closer to the population, a key development issue. This study quantifies as well as maps this phenomenon. The results highlight a high degree of variability throughout the region.

Table 1.2
Demographic sources available in 2013

Country	Census date basis for 2015 update	Population census dates
Benin	2013	2013 (p), 2006 (x), 2002, 1992, 1979
Mauritania	2013	2013 (p), 2000, 1988, 1976
Niger	2011	2012 (p), 2011(*), 2001, 1988, 1977
Nigeria	2011	2011 (e), 2006, 1991, 1963, 1952, 1931
Cabo Verde	2010	2010, 2000, 1990,1980, 1970, 1960, 1950
Ghana	2010 (provisional)	2010, 2000, 1984, 1970, 1960, 1948
Togo	2010 (provisonal)	2010, 1981, 1970, 1959
Guinea-Bissau	2009	2009, 1991, 1979, 1960, 1950
Mali	2009	2009, 1998, 1987, 1976
Chad	2009	2009, 1993, 1968 (partiel)
Liberia	2008	2008, 1984, 1974, 1962
Burkina Faso	2006 (villages)	2006, 1996, 1985, 1975
Senegal	2006	2006 (e), 2002, 1988, 1976
Sierra Leone	2004	2004, 1985, 1974, 1963
The Gambia	2003	2003, 1993, 1983, 1973, 1963, 1951
Côte d'Ivoire	1998 (villages)	1998, 1988, 1975
Guinea	1996	1996, 1983, 1958

Note: (p) Partial results, disaggregated only for higher levels of the territorial subdivisions; (x) Electoral census; (*) Preparation of the Population and housing census 2012; (e) Official estimate (usually simple projections);
Source: e-Geopolis – SWAC/OECD 2015

1.5 CONSTRAINTS IN EVALUATING THE TOTAL NATIONAL POPULATION

The method developed by e-Geopolis attempts to establish reliable estimates of the population of agglomerations; it does not, however, allow to evaluate a country's total population. Yet these data are essential as they are the denominator of many indicators, such as the level of urbanisation.

Population censuses are the only source of population data. No country in the region has a complete registry of vital records. Although there is reliable data for some countries, not one decade is complete at the level of the entire region. From 1950 to 2010, only Cape Verde, The Gambia and Ghana have regular and reliable sources.

Up until the 1970s, little was known about the total population in French-speaking countries, due to the lack of general censuses. The situation improved at the end of the 1970s when the first national censuses were carried out in Burkina Faso (Upper Volta, 1975), Côte d'Ivoire (1975), Mali (1976), Mauritania (1977), Senegal (1976), Benin (1979) and Guinea-Bissau (1979)[2]. These seven countries account for one quarter of the region's population. Adding the censuses carried out in Sierra Leone (1974), Liberia (1974), Togo (1970 and 1981) and the three countries cited above (Cape Verde (1970), The Gambia (1973), and Ghana (1970), it is during the 1970s

Table 1.3
Population of Burkina Faso (thousands)

Total population Burkina Faso (thousands)	1950	1960	1970	1980	1990	2000	2010
e-Geopolis	3 010	4 178	5 195	6 598	8 863	11 416	16 469
UN/WPP	4 284	4 882	5 807	7 212	9 339	12 314	16 496
USCB/IDB	4 376	4 866	5 304	6 318	8 361	11 588	16 242

Source: e-Geopolis 2013

that the population of most countries in the region was best known.

At this time, there was little statistical information on Nigeria, Chad and Guinea. The 1968 census in Chad did not cover the entire country and was never published. It was not until 1993 that there was an exhaustive overview of the population and its spatial distribution. In Guinea, the 1983 census had serious gaps and was only partially published. Only in 1996 reliable statistics became available. Censuses in Nigeria were contested several times. Nigeria, Chad and Guinea alone represent 59% of the region's population.

During the period 1990–2000, Liberia and Sierra Leone were profoundly affected by civil wars and massive population movements. Not a single census was undertaken in Togo between 1981 and 2010. Yet, the Nigerian population was best estimated in 1991. In terms of total population, 94% of the population was relatively well known in 1990.

In 2013 the biggest unknown was the population size of Côte d'Ivoire where a census had not been carried out since 1998 and where important population movements affected settlements patterns during the troubled 2000s. Given that the last census was carried out in Guinea in 1996, more than 10% of the region's population has not been counted in 15 years.

The international databases

At the global level there are two main databases: *World Population Prospects* by the United Nations (UN/WPP) and the International Database of the United States Census Bureau (USCB/IDB). The data from these two sources is available online. With regard to West Africa, there is a great disparity between the data of these two databases and between these and the results obtained by e-Geopolis.

The international databases smooth variations sometimes considered biased. Modelling exercises do not account sufficiently for national contexts. For instance, in 1950 in Burkina Faso (Upper Volta) the French administration of the AOF (Afrique de l' Ouest Francaise – French West Africa) counted 3 010 000 inhabitants, classified by cantons and regional capitals. Our estimate for Burkina Faso's urban population in 1950 is based on this document. However, the UN/WPP database enumerates 4 284 000 inhabitants and the USCB/IDB 4 376 000 (Table 1.3). It seems that the numbers are retropolated from more recent censuses with the underlying assumption that population growth was slower between 1950 and 1960 than in the 1970s due to a very high mortality rate, in particular infant mortality. Mortality then declined, and consequently increased the rate of population growth.

The major difference between the national and international sources is that the latter start with the growth rate to estimate the number of inhabitants. Meanwhile, e-Geopolis relies on the head count to compute the growth rate. The decline observed in the e-Geopolis population growth rate of Burkina Faso between 1950/60 and 1960/70 (Figure 1.1) could be explained by an acceleration in international emigration, in particular towards Côte d'Ivoire. Both hypotheses are debatable.

e-Geopolis estimates are essentially based on national data, rather than international. The reason is that in a study on urbanisation there is no point in introducing a statistical correction that does not correspond to the geographic

Figure 1.1
Average annual population growth rates in Burkina Faso 1950–2010

Source: e-Geopolis 2013

reality. Several reasons explain the statistical variations among the three sources. However, over the period the differences dwindle, particularly in relative terms as the population continues to grow.

Under-reporting

Situations of under-reporting are numerous and heterogeneous. Among the various causes, some can have a strong impact in some years and very little in others. The following list provides the most commonly observed cases of under-reporting:

- Under-reporting of nomadic populations. This occurs particularly in Saharan and Sahelo-Sudanian zones, which cover hundreds of thousands of km^2.
- Under-reporting of "young" men (15–40 years old). This frequently occurs in countries that are fighting a civil war for fear of enrolling young boys. In Chad, post-census inquiries show that families arrange for their young men to "disappear" into the brush during headcounts. The family simply states that they are living with a parent in a far off village or that they have emigrated abroad (Moriconi-Ebrard and Ratnan, 2006).
- Under-reporting of girls. François Ireton (CNRS), demographic specialist for Sudan and Egypt estimates that up to 70% of little girls were under-reported in the 1976 census in the rural districts ("Markaz") of Fayoum in Egypt. It is possible that this phenomenon also occurs in West Africa.
- Poor geographic coverage, not covering entire regions. This case was reported by Denis (2007) when preparing the South-Sudan census (2006–2007). Close to the border of the Central African Republic, forest mountain ranges and areas accessible only by foot or 2 wheelers were supposedly uninhabited in the censuses of 1955, 1973, and 1983. Experts have since met thousands of inhabitants living there for decades and maybe longer.
- Consciously forgetting some categories of the population. This occurs in very dense urban areas and particularly informal settlements of large cities. This omission can suit local governments.
- No response by some groups of inhabitants. Some political, linguistic, ethnic and religious groups refuse to be counted for various reasons such as tax, political, moral, land rights, military, etc. As communities tend

to group together geographically, this could also affect some territories more than others.

- "Residency" issues. Someone found in one place declares to be living in another or the other way around, or a head of household declares dependents who are living elsewhere. This often happens due to seasonal migration. For example in Niger, the population of Maradi doubled depending on the season (Giraut, 1999).

Impact of corrections on level of urbanisation

The causes of under-reporting should be better understood for each decade and each country. The issue is then whether to also correct the number of agglomerated population, for example depending on the causes of under-reporting. Thus, it could be that the estimation of the Burkinabe urban population in 1950 was correct and only the total population under-estimated, or the urban population could also have been under-estimated. Corrections can impact the level of urbanisation in two ways:

- If the urban population is under-estimated like the rest of the population, the population of the three Burkinabe cities of with more than 10 000 inhabitants (Ouagadougou, Bobo Dioulasso and Koudougou) would in reality be more than 40% greater. If we were to increase the population of all localities in Burkina Faso, Ouahigouya would then exceed 10 000 inhabitants. In other countries, adjusting the population of all localities would increase the number of localities exceeding the statistical "urban" threshold; many of the agglomerations would be reclassified, significantly increasing the level of urbanisation.
- If, however, only the rural population is adjusted, the level of urbanisation would fall by a third in 1950. The reason is that an increase in the rural population would make the share of urban population relative to total population fall, thereby decreasing the level of urbanisation.

Refugees and displaced persons

Population movements impact the size of some agglomerations that act as "refuges", making national and regional urban networks denser. The Africapolis II conclusions are pertinent to West Africa. In January 2012, UNHCR counted 327 000 refugees and 127 000 internally displaced persons, essentially in Côte d'Ivoire (UNHCR 2012). Contrary to Africapolis I & II, refugee camps are included in the 2013 inventory of agglomerations. The countries concerned are Chad (15 camps) and Liberia (2 camps).

In three countries, Côte d'Ivoire, Liberia and Chad, refugee populations seem to have impacted on the densification of urban networks. In Côte d'Ivoire, one study on urban refugees estimates that 80% of the 500 000 displaced persons in 2002, primarily from the country's northern regions, are living in urban areas, mainly in Abidjan. However, since the signing of the Ouagadougou Peace Agreement in 2007, there have been returnees (Lyytinen, 2009). Few figures exist on the impact on the size of medium-sized towns (Dekoué, Guiglio, Danané). However, some agglomerations and settlements along the border between Côte d'Ivoire and Liberia will see long term changes if refugees settle there permanently. At the beginning of 2011, 96% of 70 000 Ivorian refugees in Liberia lived in 76 villages in a barely urbanised region (UNHCR 2012). Agglomerations could emerge here, similar to the border areas of Chad.

The civil war and growth of Monrovia

The two civil wars of Liberia (1989–1996 and 1999–2003) caused the death of 200 000 people and led to the displacement of one million inhabitants, a third of the population at the time of the ceasefire (Williams, 2011). The major population movements resulted in demographic instability in numerous Liberian localities. The country's second largest city in 1984, Camp IV with 49 400 inhabitants, was destroyed in 2003. By 2005 its population had fallen to 1 100. Several other cities experienced a similar decline. The provisional results of the 2008 census provide figures of displaced persons by *county*. Among the two million enumerated displaced persons in Liberia, 746 000 resettled and 95 000 did not, leaving more than half of the displaced persons unaccounted for. At the height of the fighting, Monrovia's population was estimated to be between 1 and 1.5 million (UN Habitat, cited by Williams, 2011). According to our estimates Monrovia counted 1.2 million inhabitants in 2010. While in other countries, the growth rate of metropolises is slowing down (primarily due to a decline in the rate of natural increase), Monrovia is since the beginning of the 1980s following an opposite trend. From 1980 (the year of the first coup d'État) to 2000, Monrovia's growth rate was double that of other agglomerations in the country. The state has since advocated for displaced persons to return to their region of origin with some success, but allows them the possibility to stay. Similar to other war refuge cities like Khartoum (Sudan) and Luanda (Angola), Monrovia's informal housing areas are inhabited by displaced persons with likely consequences on access to services and land security.

The effects on urban networks: The example of Chad

The effects are linked to the long presence of refugee camps in sparsely populated areas and initially poorly integrated with the rest of the territory. In Chad, twelve camps have been set up since 2004 along the border with Darfur (Sudan) and between 2003 and 2008 six along the border with the Central African Republic. The population of the camps along the Sudanese border in 2010 ranged from 12 000 to 32 000, in a region where the only other agglomerations are Irida (42 000 inhabitants), Adré (16 000 inhabitants) and Tine Djangarba (16 000 inhabitants). Studies carried out in the Horn of Africa consider the camps as "towns", recognising their vitality and economic activity as well as their trade links with urban centres. The length of presence is a main explanatory element (10 to 20 years). Aid flows also tend to be provided for the host communities while proposing micro-economic agricultural and revenue generating projects to refugees. The permanence of camps changes the urban geography and is an element of regional integration with neighbouring countries (economic and populations flows).

Differences in surface area ... and density

There are some significant differences among sources concerning countries' surface area which consequently affect the calculation of population densities. Table 1.4 compares World Bank data to the sum of the administrative units from national data.

In order to understand and interpret these discrepancies:

- It should be noted that not one West African country provides land registry surface area data at the national level. In 2013, the first national geo-referenced land registry was being carried out in Cape Verde (surface area of 4 033 km², 0.05% of the regional surface area).
- Surface area is calculated based on maps. There are significant differences in the choice of calculation method and projections, especially in the larger countries.
- Some countries include water bodies in their surface area and others do not. However, these are not insignificant. Lakes, lagoons and dams in the 17 countries cover an area of 37 643 km², equivalent to a country like Guinea-Bissau.
- Some of the differences in the table are also due to rounding.

The biggest difference is in The Gambia and can be explained by whether or not the river's estuaries are included. In Ghana, the difference is due to the inclusion of the Akosombo dam (7 884 km²), which is not part of any district and was therefore not included in the second column. The surface area of Guinea-Bissau varies by +/- 8 120 km² between low tide (36 120 km²) and high tide (28 000 km²).

Table 1.4

Differences in countries' surface area World Bank vs. national sources (in km²)

Country	World Bank	National sources	% difference
Gambia	11 300	8 613	-31.0
Liberia	111 370	99 025	-12.0
Ghana	239 460	230 680	-4.0
Burkina Faso	274 200	270 764	-1.0
Chad	1 284 000	1 274 413	-1.0
Côte d'Ivoire	322 460	320 803	-1.0
Mali	1 240 000	1 238 192	0.0
Guinea	245 857	245 790	0.0
Cabo Verde	4 033	4 033	0.0
Sierra Leone	71 740	71 740	0.0
Togo	56 785	56 785	0.0
Benin	112 620	112 622	0.0
Guinea-Bissau	36 120	36 124	0.0
Senegal	196 190	196 712	0.0
Niger	1 267 000	1 271 947	0.0
Mauritania	1 030 700	1 035 000	0.0
Nigeria	923 768	937 052	1.0
Total	**7 427 603**	**7 410 295**	**0.0**

Source: e-Geopolis 2013; World Bank 2013

Table 1.5

Country population estimates – e-Geopolis, UN/WPP and USCB/IDB (thousands)

e-Geopolis	**1950**	**1960**	**1970**	**1980**	**1990**	**2000**	**2010**
TOTAL	62 031	77 432	99 723	133 516	175 554	235 301	**322 579**
Benin	1 572	2 237	2 709	3 460	4 689	6 411	9 000
Burkina Faso	3 010	4 178	5 195	6 598	8 863	11 416	16 469
Cabo Verde	150	200	271	296	**355**	435	492
Chad	2 242	2 899	3 393	4 387	5 766	8 173	**11 755**
Côte d'Ivoire	2 422	3 161	5 294	8 042	11 538	15 788	19 658
Gambia	**276**	306	436	628	919	1 262	1 728
Ghana	**5 544**	6 727	8 559	11 029	14 240	18 412	24 223
Guinea	2 250	2 944	4 133	5 445	**6 549**	7 937	9 982
Guinea-Bissau	509	525	487	785	952	1 239	**1 598**
Liberia	820	955	1 354	1 867	**2 401**	**2 965**	3 663
Mali	3 400	4 071	5 094	6 727	8 223	10 630	15 178
Mauritania	847	1 007	1 241	1 530	1 960	2 508	3 163
Niger	2 164	2 867	4 008	5 616	7 609	10 604	15 512
Nigeria	31 800	39 230	49 300	65 700	86 950	119 350	**166 125**
Senegal	2 060	2 529	3 776	**5 648**	7 250	9 479	12 053
Sierra Leone	1 915	2 116	2 519	3 137	3 850	**4 161**	5 868
Togo	1 050	1 480	1 954	2 621	3 440	4 531	6 112

Note: Maximum values are in bold.

Table 1.5

Country population estimates – e-Geopolis, UN/WPP and USCB/IDB (thousands) *(cont.)*

UN/WPP	1950	1960	1970	1980	1990	2000	2010
TOTAL	**72 874**	**88 561**	**111 025**	**144 317**	**189 060**	**244 673**	316 537
Benin	**2 255**	**2 420**	**2 850**	**3 611**	**4 794**	6 543	8 882
Burkina Faso	4 284	**4 882**	**5 807**	**7 212**	**9 339**	**12 314**	**16 496**
Cabo Verde	**178**	**211**	**274**	**300**	351	**441**	502
Chad	2 429	2 954	3 656	**4 554**	**6 030**	**8 248**	11 259
Côte d'Ivoire	2 630	**3 638**	5 416	8 501	**12 551**	16 633	19 818
Gambia	271	**373**	459	630	**967**	1 299	1 731
Ghana	4 981	6 742	8 682	10 923	14 844	**19 242**	**24 512**
Guinea	**3 094**	**3 541**	**4 154**	4 407	5 775	**8 373**	10 021
Guinea-Bissau	518	593	603	**835**	**1 020**	1 245	1 521
Liberia	**911**	**1 116**	**1 440**	**1 923**	2 132	2 854	**4 005**
Mali	**4 638**	**5 248**	**6 034**	**7 246**	**8 687**	**11 317**	**15 395**
Mauritania	657	854	1 134	1 518	**1 999**	**2 647**	**3 466**
Niger	2 462	3 250	4 373	5 871	7 797	**10 937**	**15 533**
Nigeria	**37 860**	**45 926**	**57 357**	**75 543**	**97 859**	124 102	159 022
Senegal	2 416	3 048	4 096	5 414	7 250	**9 519**	**12 450**
Sierra Leone	1 895	2 187	2 593	3 162	3 987	4 147	**5 871**
Togo	**1 395**	**1 578**	**2 097**	**2 667**	3 678	4 812	6 053

Note: Maximum values are in bold.

Table 1.5

Country population estimates – e-Geopolis, UN/WPP and USCB/IDB (thousands) *(cont.)*

USCB/IDB	1950	1960	1970	1980	1990	2000	2010
TOTAL	66 889	83 941	108 770	142 991	187 715	242 524	317 128
Benin	1 673	2 055	2 620	3 458	4 705	**6 619**	**9 056**
Burkina Faso	**4 376**	4 866	5 304	6 317	8 361	11 588	16 242
Cabo Verde	146	197	269	296	340	430	**509**
Chad	**2 608**	**3 042**	**3 727**	4 522	5 841	7 943	10 543
Côte d'Ivoire	**2 860**	3 576	**5 579**	**8 593**	12 491	**16 885**	**21 059**
Gambia	271	352	**485**	**652**	951	**1 357**	**1 755**
Ghana	5 297	**6 958**	**8 789**	**11 153**	**15 549**	18 981	23 571
Guinea	2 586	3 026	3 643	**4 447**	6 118	8 350	10 324
Guinea-Bissau	**573**	**617**	**620**	789	996	**1 279**	1 565
Liberia	824	1 055	1 397	1 857	2 139	2 601	3 685
Mali	3 688	4 495	5 546	6 868	8 487	10 788	14 583
Mauritania	**1 006**	**1 117**	**1 289**	**1 545**	1 925	2 501	3 205
Niger	**3 271**	**3 913**	**4 841**	**6 093**	**7 825**	10 725	15 270
Nigeria	31 797	41 550	55 590	74 829	96 690	**124 207**	161 605
Senegal	**2 654**	**3 270**	**4 318**	5 611	**7 348**	9 469	12 323
Sierra Leone	**2 087**	**2 396**	**2 789**	**3 335**	**4 228**	3 809	5 246
Togo	1 172	1 456	1 964	2 626	**3 721**	4 992	**6 587**

Note: Maximum values are in bold.

Sources: e-Geopolis 2013: estimates based on the geometric interpolation from the series of available official head counts (colonial and national post-independence); UN/WPP: "World Population Prospects the 2011 revision"; USCB/IDB: US Census Bureau "International Database".

NOTES \\\

1 *See Africapolis I and II for more details.*

2 *Guinea-Bissau is a Portuguese speaking country.*

Bibliography

Denis, E. (2007), "Inégalités régionales et rébellions au Soudan", *Outre-Terre*, No. 20, Éditions Erès, http://dx.doi.org/10.3917/oute.020.0151.

Giraut F. (1999), "Retour du refoulé et effet chef-lieu: Analyse d'une refonte politico-administrative virtuelle au Niger", *Graphigéo*, Pôle de Recherche pour l'Organisation et la Diffusion de l'Information Géographique UMR Prodig, Paris, www.prodig.cnrs.fr/IMG/pdf/1999-7.pdf.

Lyytinen, E. (2009), "A tale of three cities: Internal displacement, urbanization and humanitarian action in Abidjan, Khartoum and Mogadishu", *New Issues in Refugee Research*, Research Paper No. 173, UNHCR, www.unhcr.org/4a1d33e96.html.

Moriconi-Ebrard, F. and N. Ratnan (2006), "Population", in *Atlas du Tchad*, Éditions du Jaguar, Paris.

UNHCR (2012), "Regional operations profile West Africa", Office of the United Nations High Commissioner for Refugees, www.unhcr.org/pages/49e45a9c6.html (accessed 29 November 2012).

Williams, R.C. (2011), "Beyond Squatters' Rights: Durable Solutions and Development-induced Displacement in Monrovia, Liberia", *Norwegian Refugee Council Thematic Report*, Oslo, www.nrc.no/arch/_img/9195244.pdf.

Chapter 2

Demographic growth and the spread of agglomerations in West Africa

2.1 RE-ACCELERATION OF URBAN POPULATION GROWTH

In the ten years between 2000 and 2010 the urban population grew by 48 million people, reaching 133 million; this represents an increase of close to 60%. The average annual urban population growth rate rose to 4.6%, up from 4.1% in the previous decade (1990–2000). The 4.6% urban population growth rate equals the average of the last 30 years (Figure 2.1).

Eleven countries saw an increase in their urban population growth rate during the last decade; in seven of these countries growth over the last decade was faster than the average for 1980 to 2010. Chad had the highest average annual growth rate at 6.8%, followed by Mali (6.2%), Burkina Faso (6.1%) and Niger (5%). Chad also saw the fastest acceleration in the rate of growth compared to the previous decade, increasing by 1.9 percentage points, followed by Guinea-Bissau (1.6), Mauritania (1.5) and Liberia (1.4).

The Gambia saw the greatest deceleration in the urban population growth rate, from 6.6% (the highest during 1990–2000) to 3.9%; followed by Cape Verde (-1.5 percentage points), Guinea (-1.2) and Côte d'Ivoire (-0.9).

However, urban growth over the last decades is lower than during the post-independence period. Between 1950 and 1980, the regional average growth rate was 6.4%. In addition, in no country was the growth rate of the last decade greater than the long-term average between 1950 and 2010, except Guinea-Bissau and Mali.

In some countries the observed acceleration in urban population growth can be explained by an increase in total population growth. While it was thought that demographic growth in West Africa was declining, the results of the most recent censuses, Mali 2009 and Niger 2012, indicate otherwise. Population growth has also been on the rise in Benin (2002–2013) and Nigeria (1991–2006). The renewed pick up in population growth still needs to be confirmed in the other countries. However, this increase should be transitory since it can be explained by strong reductions in mortality rate, especially infant mortality. These fluctuations are part of the demographic transition (Figure 2.2). Yet, it has an effect on urban population growth without being directly linked to economy driven urbanisation processes. At the same time, the drop in the infant mortality rate can be the result of improved access to health services brought about by urbanisation.

2.2 CONTINUED INCREASE IN THE LEVEL OF URBANISATION

The regional level of urbanisation increased from 36% in 2000 to 41% in 2010. Seven countries have an urbanisation rate close to 50%: Côte d'Ivoire 48%, The Gambia 48%, Cape Verde 47%, Nigeria (46%), Senegal 46%, Togo 46% and Ghana 45%. At only 18%, Niger remained one of the least urbanised countries in the world, comparable with Ethiopia and Burundi (see Africapolis II).

Nigeria's urbanisation dynamics greatly influence the regional average. Excluding Nigeria, the regional level of urbanisation drops to 36%. In 1950, Senegal (21%) was the most urbanised country in West Africa, when the regional level of urbanisation was 9%. Urbanisation levels are less homogeneous today than they were sixty years ago. This is a cumulative effect of the imbalances of demographic and economic growth, the development of some coastal metropolises turned towards the global economy, and differences in territorial and land planning policies as well as settlement patterns.

Figure 2.1

Urban population growth rate 1990–2010 (compound annual growth)

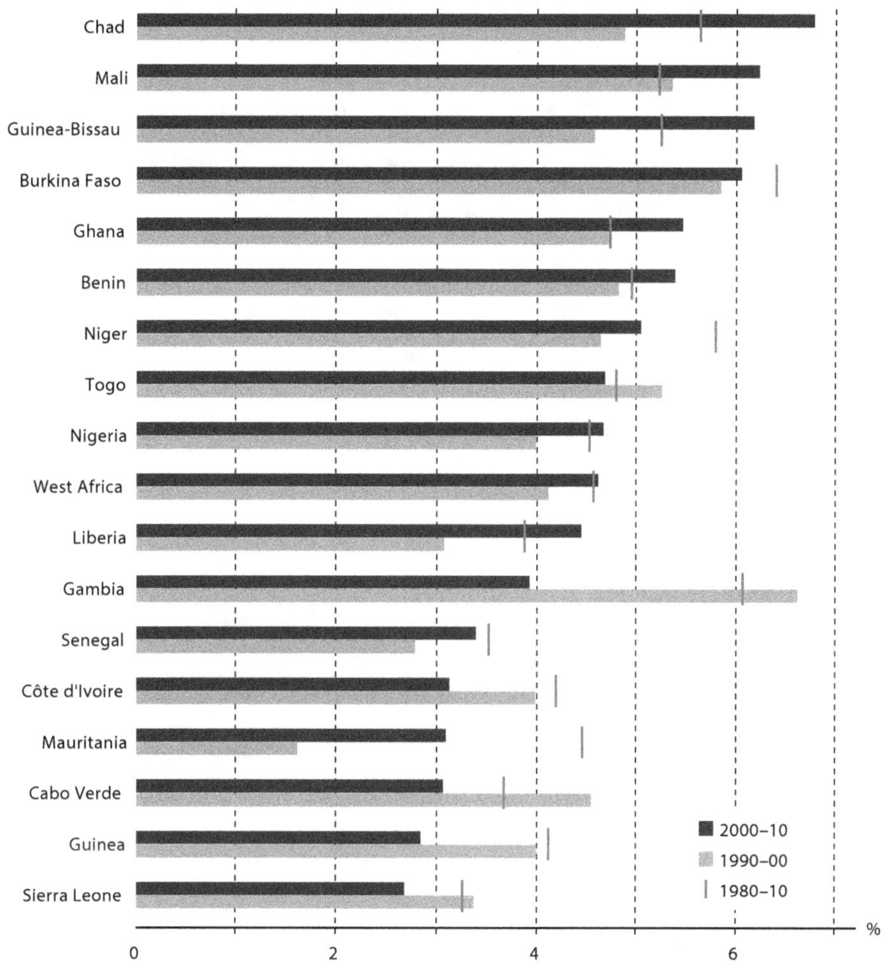

Source: e-Geopolis - SWAC/OECD 2015

Figure 2.2

The pace of urbanisation and the level of urbanisation in 2010 (calculated by the ratio U/R)

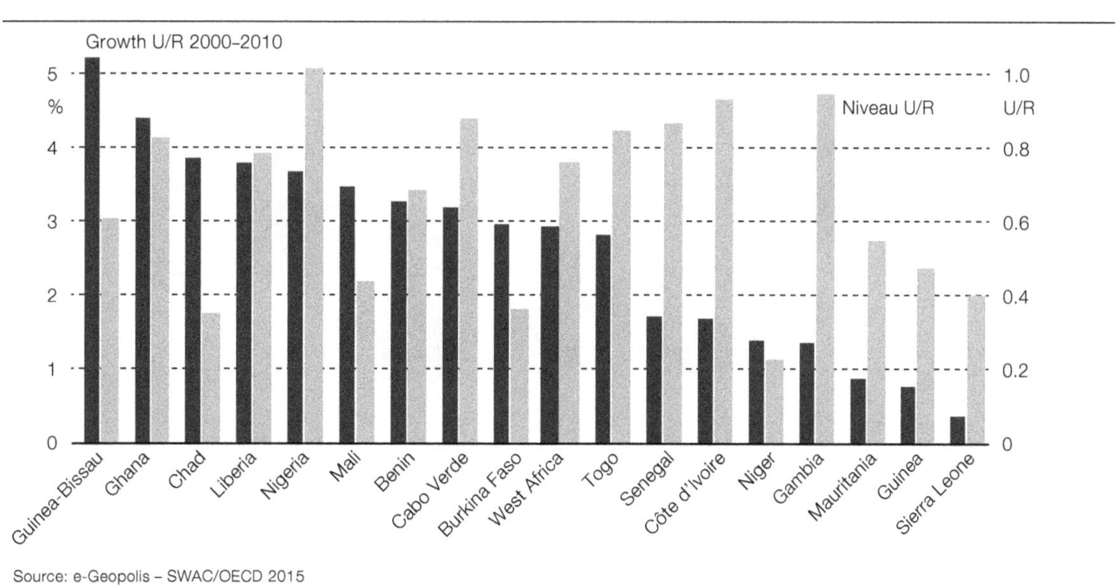

Source: e-Geopolis – SWAC/OECD 2015

Map 2.1

Level of urbanisation 1950, 1980 and 2010

Source: e-Geopolis – SWAC/OECD 2015

2.3 DENSIFICATION AND DIFFUSION OF THE URBAN NETWORK

In 2010, 133 million urban dwellers in West Africans lived in the 1 947 agglomerations with at least 10 000 inhabitants, which is 530 more than in 2000[1]. In 1970 West Africa had a total of only 493 agglomerations, highlighting the extent of the densification of the urban network. Today the region counts 22 metropolises with over one million inhabitants, as compared to 10 in 2000. These 22 cities accommodate 54.4 million inhabitants, which is almost the same as the region's entire urban population only twenty years earlier (56 million in 1990).

In the middle of the 20th century, urban areas were concentrated along the Gulf of Guinea, and in particular in the Yoruba area of Nigeria. Today, West Africa's urban network is much denser and expanded throughout the entire region (Maps 2.2 and 2.3), including the Sahara desert *sensu stricto*, where twenty or so towns have appeared (Niger, Mali, Mauritania, Chad) despite an overall low population density. Large urban centres previously confined to the coastline are now also present inland, national capitals, secondary towns like Bobo Dioulasso (Burkina Faso), Bouaké (Côte d'Ivoire), Touba (Senegal), Kumasi (Ghana) and several large agglomerations in Nigeria. The number of small agglomerations has multiplied spectacularly throughout the region.

Figure 2.3
Number of agglomerations (10 000 or more inhabitants) 1960, 1980, 2010

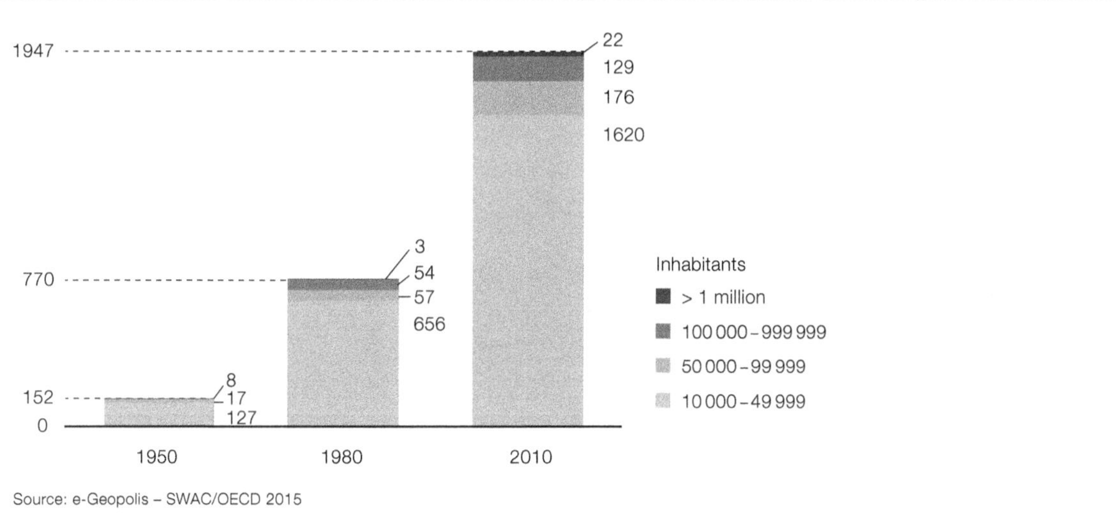

Source: e-Geopolis – SWAC/OECD 2015

Map 2.2

Distribution and size of urban agglomerations in 1960

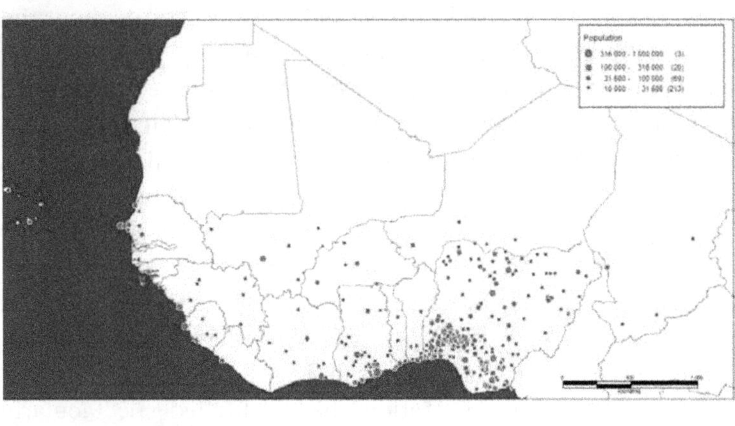

Source: e-Geopolis – SWAC/OECD 2015

Map 2.3

Distribution and size of urban agglomerations in 2010

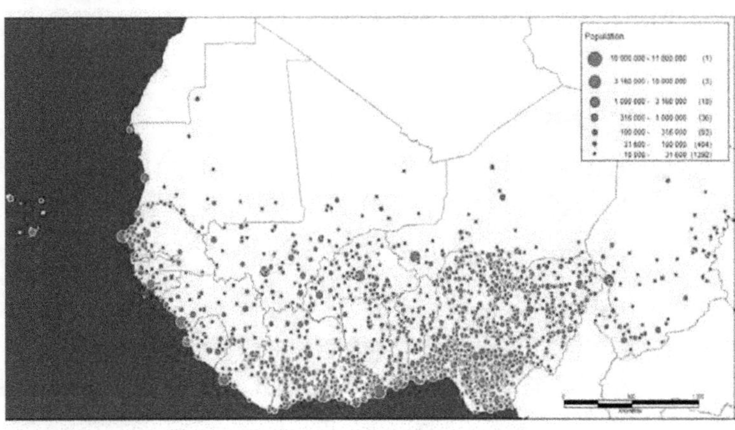

Source: e-Geopolis – SWAC/OECD 2015

2.4 COASTAL AND URBAN CORRIDORS

In the 2010 report, "The state of the world's cities 2010–2011: Bridging the urban divide", UN-Habitat underscores how "urban development corridors" stimulate the local economy through the real estate sector, development of land and business and better interconnection between urban centres. Among the corridors of international standing, almost at the same level as the industrial corridor of Mumbai-Delhi and Beijing–Tokyo, the report cites the 600 km corridor of Ibadan–Lagos–Accra as the economic engine of West Africa. On a very broad scale, one could talk of the coastal corridor, or rather the "parallel-to-the-coast" corridor.

The notion of regional integration is interesting because during the colonial period, movement in West Africa was north-south like a "wide-toothed comb". The penetrating roads, the main development areas, ran perpendicular to the coastline. The corridor described here is the reversal of historic trade and settlement patterns. However, focusing on the coastal area in the strictest sense, Ibadan could not be included. How we think of the urban concept is also important. The Ibadan–Lagos–Accra corridor can be considered as much a settlement corridor as an urban corridor, given its inclusion of very dense rural areas. At the same time, the high densities

Table 2.1
The coastal urban network in 2010

Country	Share of urban population	Number of agglomerations
Cabo Verde	87%	2
Gambia	82%	5
Senegal	78%	9
Guinea-Bissau	76%	1
Liberia	75%	2
Mauritania	74%	2
Sierra Leone	56%	2
Togo	53%	2
Côte d'Ivoire	47%	11
Guinea	47%	2
Ghana	41%	18
Benin	36%	5
West Africa	25%	77
Nigeria	17%	16

Source: e-Geopolis – SWAC/OECD 2015.

also explain the emergence of conurbations, based on the substratum of dense population units (hamlets, villages, small agglomerations), and further sustain the corridor's future influence and economic potential.

Urban or not, coastal or not, this corridor is an important part of the regional urban system. Although the number of medium and small agglomerations remains limited, they represent 40% of all coastal agglomerations identified by e-Geopolis. The 2000 km coastal axis that links Port Harcourt to Abidjan accounts today for two thirds of regional trade between ECOWAS countries (ECOWAS/OECD, 2005). According to UN-Habitat, if the two criteria to form a development corridor are met – namely the presence of two major urban centres and the capacity to attract flows of goods, services and population – only political constraints could slow its future expansion to Abidjan and beyond. The presence of secondary agglomerations, particularly Cape Coast and Sekondi-Takoradi in Ghana, situated along the 400 km linking Accra to Abidjan, and the emergence of small agglomerations along the Ivorian coastline, can only encourage this expansion.

The western part of the Atlantic coastline does not yet have the attributes needed for a development corridor. The coastline is not an axis of major historical movement and metropolises are poorly linked to each other. Furthermore, the prolonged political crises and conflicts in Liberia, Sierra Leone and Côte d'Ivoire, as well as the Casamance conflict, still hinder trade and the movement of people. The renewed dynamism of the Mano River Union (Côte d'Ivoire, Guinea, Liberia, Sierra Leone) could, however, provide new stimulus.

Non-coastal urban corridors

In 2008, the Africapolis I study emphasised that the proliferation of agglomerations would take shape along the axes perpendicular to the coastline: Dakar-Touba, Abidjan-Bouaké, Accra-Kumasi, Lomé-Kara, Cotonou/Porto Novo-Abomey, Lagos-Ibadan. It would follow a process of linear urbanisation linked to the major North-South routes, following historic trade corridors such as the Maradi–Katsina–Kano axis and various north-south trade networks linking different agro-climatic zones. Today, international organisations recognise the role of these non-coastal development corridors (UN-Habitat, 2010). For example, some of the most important secondary agglomerations of Côte d'Ivoire and Burkina Faso (Yamoussoukro, Bouaké, Korhogo, Banfora, Bobo-Dioulasso), as well as numerous smaller agglomerations, have developed along the Abidjan–Ouagadougou corridor.

2.5 CONTRASTED GROWTH BETWEEN METROPOLISES AND SMALL AGGLOMERATIONS

"Megacities" remain modest in size

Long considered under-urbanised, West Africa no longer fits this description. The level of urbanisation has increased significantly and the region boasts several very large cities. In 2010, Lagos was the largest city in sub-Saharan Africa in terms of inhabitants and ranked 27th in the world, just above Paris and London (Table 2.2). With its 10.6 million inhabitants it is still much smaller than the large Asian agglomerations. Similarly, in terms of surface area, Lagos is still a "small" megacity, 2.5 times smaller than London or Paris… but also 2.5 times denser.

Table 2.3 confirms the end of the demographic explosion in metropolises (Moriconi-Ebrard, 1996). There is a decline in growth rates in most of the metropolises. Even if growth rates remain high, they are below the records set during 1960 to 1970. An increase in an agglomeration's growth rate does not necessarily indicate an attraction stemming from the agglomeration.

Firstly, the acceleration in population growth revealed by the latest censuses in Mali (2009) and Niger (2012) appears to be impacting urban growth rates. Secondly the growth patterns of metropolises can further explain the observed trends. Analysis of satellite images shows the spatial sprawl of agglomerations such as Cotonou, Nouakchott, and Ouagadougou. At the local level, this sprawl is contrary to concentration since by definition it is a centrifugal force. At the national level, however, it is seen as the forming of large metropolitan areas in the process of agglomerating (Accra, Abidjan, Banjul, Dakar) and becoming conurbations. Onitsha's growth rate is an illustration: the overall growth rate is a combination of the growth rate of the city itself (about 3% per year) and the spatial expansion of the central agglomeration leading to a merging with villages at the periphery and with initially separate agglomerations.

The agglomerations in Table 2.3 are not selected based on *absolute* demographic size but rather *relative* to an urban system. The share of capital cities' population in the total urban population indicates a decoupling of the metropolitan areas growth from national urbanisation (Figure 2.4). This phenomenon, not specific to Africa, leads to a centralisation of urban systems (Europe: France, Ireland, Greece; Asia: Thailand, Philippines; and Latin America: Argentina, Chile, Guatemala) (Moriconi-Ebrard, 1993). Except in Nigeria, at least one third and up to three quarters of the total urban population live in the national metropolis.

Bissau, with only 458 000 inhabitants, is Guinea Bissau's uncontested metropolis, accounting for three quarters of the country's urban population. Guinea Bissau's second agglomeration, Gabú, has only 61 000 inhabitants. In comparison, Abeokuta in Nigeria is of a similar size (460 000 inhabitants), but ranks 42nd in Nigeria and is trivial in size with respect to the national urban system. However, smaller agglomerations located in very rural areas, in isolated desert areas, within a particular natural environment or capitals of socio-linguistic and religious groups, can appear as metropolises. Genuine national metropolises are the result of centralisation, a political process that prevailed in most West African countries, in some cases prior to independence.

Table 2.2
Global agglomerations of 10 million or more inhabitants (2010)

Rank	Agglomeration	Country	Population (millions)	Urbanised surface area (km²)	Density (inhab/km²)	Last source year
1	Shanghai	China	94.5	22.6	4.2	2010
2	Shenzhen	China	44.4	5.3	8.4	2010
3	Tokyo	Japan	39.8	4.2	9.5	2010
4	New York	United States	27.8	20.4	1.4	2010
5	Delhi	India	23.3	1.4	16.6	2011
6	Jakarta	Indonesia	22.6	2.2	10.3	2010
7	Seoul	Korea	20.5	1.2	17.1	2010
8	Manila	Philippines	20.1	1.1	18.3	2010
9	Karachi	Pakistan	19.6	800.0	24.5	2010
10	São Paulo	Brazil	18.9	2.0	9.5	2010
11	Mexico City	Mexico	18.1	1.7	10.6	2010
12	Cochin	India	18.0	9.0	2.0	2011
13	Calcutta	India	17.2	1.9	9.1	2011
14	Beijing	China	16.7	2.4	7.0	2010
15	Mumbai	India	16.5	470.0	35.1	2011
16	Cairo	Egypt	15.7	1.3	12.1	2006
17	Dhaka	Bangladesh	15.7	1.1	14.3	2011
18	Los Angeles	United States	15.4	7.1	2.2	2010
19	Osaka	Japan	14.5	2.9	5.0	2010
20	Bangkok	Thailand	14.2	3.2	4.4	2010
21	Moscow	Russia	14.0	1.9	7.4	2010
22	Ho Chin Minh City	Viet Nam	13.8	3.0	4.6	2009
23	Istanbul	Turkey	13.5	1.1	12.3	2011
24	Teheran	Iran	12.1	1.9	6.4	2011
25	Rio de Janeiro	Brazil	11.4	1.6	7.1	2010
26	Buenos Aires	Argentina	11.2	2.5	4.5	2010
27	Lagos	Nigeria	10.6	860.0	12.3	2006
28	Paris	France	10.5	1.9	5.5	2009
29	London	UK	10.2	2.2	4.6	2011
30	Lahore	Pakistan	10.0	370.0	27.0	1998

Source: e-Geopolis 2013

Table 2.3

National metropolises: Size and growth rates

Country – Metropolis	2010	2000	1990	1980	Growth rate 2000–10	Growth rate 1980–2010
Nigeria – Lagos	**10 590 000**	7 178 000	4 865 000	2 690 000	4.0	4.7
Nigeria – Onitsha	**6 280 000**	1 450 000	620 000	392 000	15.8	9.7
Côte d'Ivoire – Abidjan[1]	**3 967 000**	3 043 326	2 107 460	1 251 272	2.7	3.9
Ghana – Accra	**3 630 000**	2 015 649	1 185 614	854 659	6.1	4.9
Nigeria – Kano	**3 150 000**	2 032 000	1 311 000	715 000	4.5	5.1
Senegal – Dakar	**2 562 152**	1 964 179	1 586 138	967 051	2.7	3.3
Mali – Bamako	**2 270 000**	1 234 696	747 828	494 032	6.3	5.2
Burkina Faso – Ouagadougou	**1 908 000**	965 521	548 326	264 680	7.0	6.8
Togo – Lome[2]	**1 449 000**	917 378	609 223	405 512	4.7	4.3
Guinea – Conakry[1]	**1 409 000**	1 161 551	895 821	589 594	2.0	2.9
Liberia – Monrovia	**1 170 000**	745 539	541 268	367 152	4.6	3.9
Niger – Niamey	**1 170 000**	660 907	427 810	260 227	5.9	5.1
Benin – Cotonou	**1 159 000**	845 680	529 599	344 021	3.2	4.1
Chad – N'Djamena[3]	**1 006 000**	694 435	459 829	284 685	3.8	4.3
Sierra Leone – Freetown	**929 000**	763 323	529 941	315 255	2.0	3.7
Mauritania – Nouakchott	**744 000**	558 195	416 956	184 139	2.9	4.8
Gambia – Serrekunda	**603 000**	395 969	206 399	84 322	4.3	6.8
Guinea-Bissau – Bissau	**458 000**	298 818	182 832	115 636	4.4	4.7
Cabo Verde – Praia	**130 271**	96 734	61 644	38 125	3.0	4.2

[1] 2010 figures based on censuses prior to 2000.

[2] The agglomeration of Lomé spills into Ghana (Aflao), unaccounted for in this table.

[3] N'Djaména is agglomerated to Kousséri, Cameroon, to which it is linked by a bridge over the Chari River. Only N'Djamena's population is included in this table.

Source: e-Geopolis – SWAC/OECD 2015

Figure 2.4
Share of the metropolitan population in total urban population (in %, 2010)

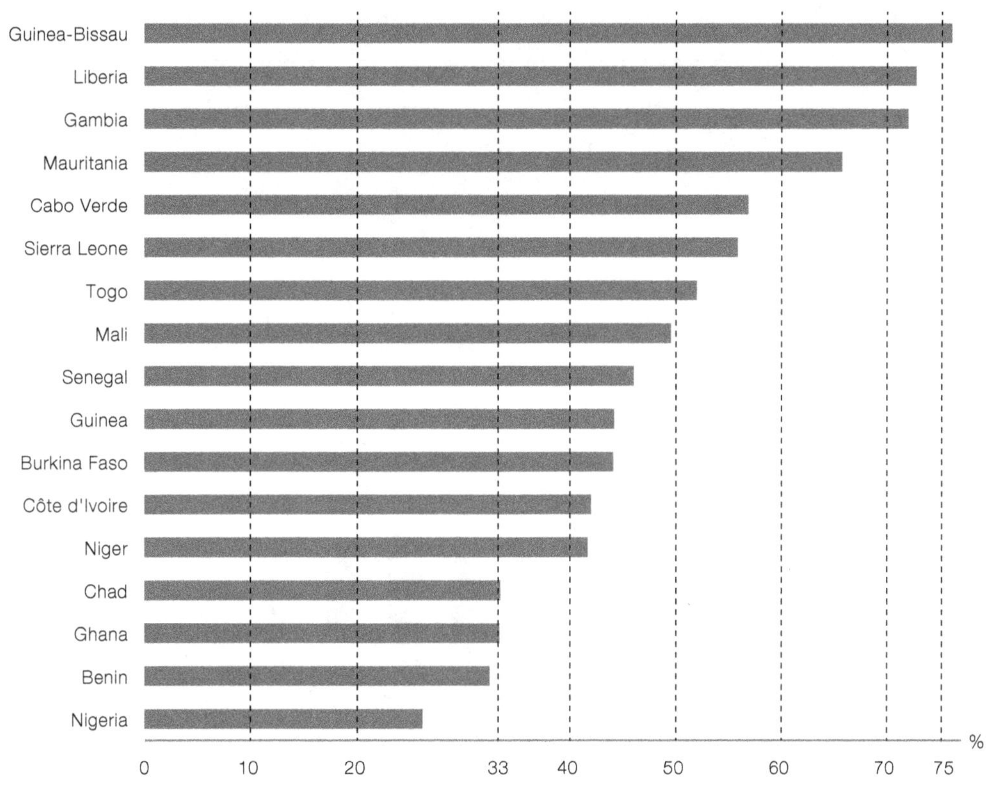

Note: In Nigeria three cities are considered (Lagos, Onitsha and Kano).
Source: e-Geopolis - SWAC/OECD 2015

Among the various possible levels, an urban network is best thought of at the national level, in particular for reasons such as sharing control of movement at borders, national structure of infrastructure and communication systems (e.g. mobile phone subscriptions and cards) and national currencies[2]. Centralisation dynamics can also appear within a stable hinterland of a national territory, yet internal administrative subdivisions have far more delicate borders. All these conditions taken together contribute to what is termed a "national urban system".

Centralisation implies the selection of an agglomeration that concentrates modern equipment and services, most skilled jobs and political, financial and media centres. It becomes the trade hub between a more or less captive hinterland and international trade, whose intensity is constantly increasing in a globalised and liberalised world economy. In some cases, generally large countries (not in West Africa) and/or federally structured countries, two, three, or more national metropolises can exist. In Nigeria, three settlement areas testify to the coexistence prior to independence of metropolises. These include the West Colony, centred around the Yoruba with Ibadan, and later Lagos; the Eastern territories, later integrated with the Colony on the Niger Delta with Onitsha; and the Northern Protectorate, centred around Kano.

In Upper Volta, Bobo Dioulasso, a genuine "port" of the territory when it was the last stop on the rail line from Abidjan, had a population greater than Ouagadougou. Post-independence, the capital Ouagadougou grew much faster and is today three times larger than Bobo-Dioulasso. Cape Verde initially had two competing cities, Praia and Mindelo, although decades later Praia now takes precedence over Mindelo.

Very high national primacies

The primacy index indicates the size of the gap between the most populated and the second agglomeration. According to the Zipf rank-size law, the biggest agglomeration should be twice

Figure 2.5
Evolution of primacy indices from 1980 to 2010

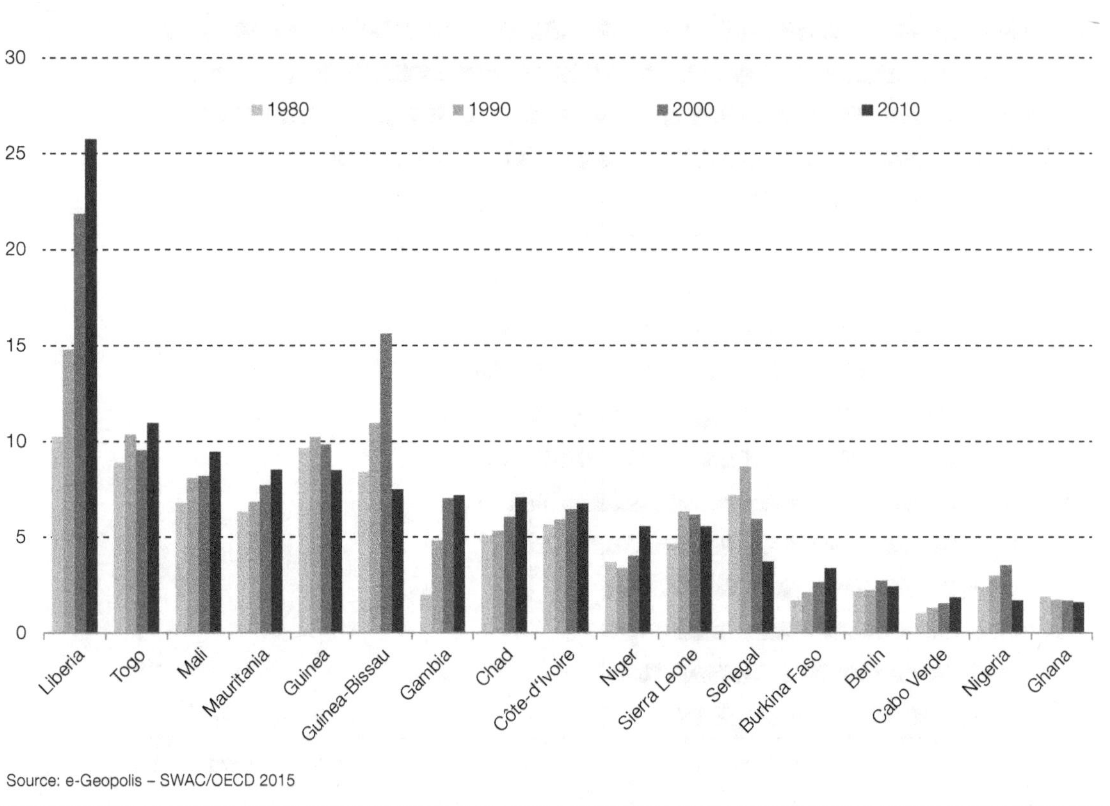

Source: e-Geopolis – SWAC/OECD 2015

as populated as the second (Zipf, 1941). Far from this model, West Africa's primacy indices are extremely high and growing in most of the countries except Ghana, Nigeria, Senegal and Sierra Leone. In Liberia and The Gambia, where the metropolises account for three quarters of the total urban population, the primacy index reached 26 and 8 respectively. In Mali and Togo, the primacy index continues to increase, around 10 in 2010 (Figure 2.5).

The lower primacy rate in Burkina Faso and Cape Verde, both having two historic metropolises, should not be misleading. In both countries the greatest discontinuity in the rank-size distribution is between the 2nd and 3rd ranked city. Bobo-Dioulasso is "only" 3.4 times less populated than the capital, but six times more populated than the 3rd ranked agglomeration, Koudougou. In Cape Verde, Mindelo, which has half the population of Praia, is four times greater than Espargos. Primacy is truly moderate in only three countries: Nigeria, Ghana and Benin.

Stability in the metropolises and instability in secondary cities

The primacy index does not only depend on the initial size of the national metropolises but also on the dynamic of other large agglomerations that could fall into this category. In many countries the same agglomeration ranks second for an extended period of time. This is true of Bouaké in Côte d'Ivoire, Kumasi in Ghana, Porto-Novo in Benin and Zinder in Niger, as well as Bobo-Dioulasso (Burkina Faso) since 1960. These urban centres play major economic or political roles at the national level. Elsewhere, the increase in the primacy index is due to instability in secondary towns.

- In Mali, four agglomerations have successively been ranked second since 1950. Kayes in 1950 and 1960, Mopti in 1970, Ségou in 1980 and 1990, and Sikasso since 2000 (Figure 2.6);
- In Senegal, Saint-Louis in 1950, Kaolack in 1960, Thiès from 1970 to 1990, and Touba since 2000;

Figure 2.6
Rank-size distribution in Mali

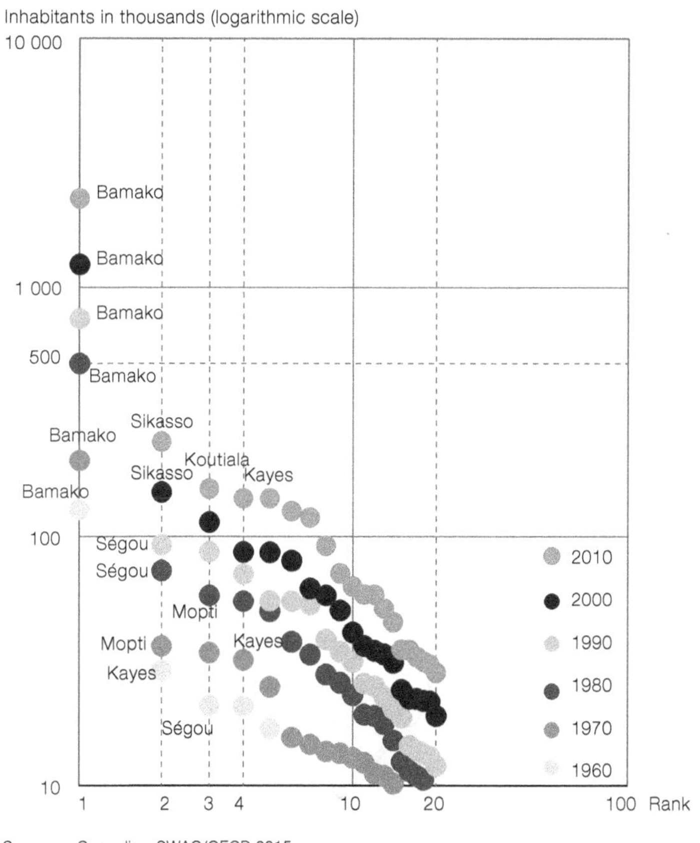

Source: e-Geopolis – SWAC/OECD 2015

- In Guinea, Kankan (1950–1990), Nzérékoré (2000) and Guéckédou (2010);
- In Chad, 2nd oscillates between Moundou (1950 and from 1990 to 2010) and Sarh (from 1960 to 1980), closely followed by Abéché which moved to 3rd in 2010;
- In Nigeria, Lagos in 1950, Ibadan in 1960–1990, Kano in 2000 then Onitsha in 2010;
- In Sierra Leone, Bo (1950 and 1960), Koidu (1970–1990), and Bo again in 2000 and 2010;
- In Mauritania, the instability in secondary cities is less marked with Nouadhibou replacing Kaédi as from 1980 and remaining 2nd since.
- Finally, The Gambia shares with Oman the unique case in which its capital city, Banjul, has fallen dramatically in the hierarchy. Banjul's expansion is naturally constrained and its territory saturated. Serrekunda, the country's largest agglomeration, is in reality only a spatial projection of Banjul. Functionally, Serrekunda was formed from the merging of a group of outlying areas separated from the city centre. Thus the rise in primacy is due to growth of the capital city as well as by the weakness of other secondary agglomerations.

Figure 2.7
Rank-size distribution of urban agglomerations, 1950–2010

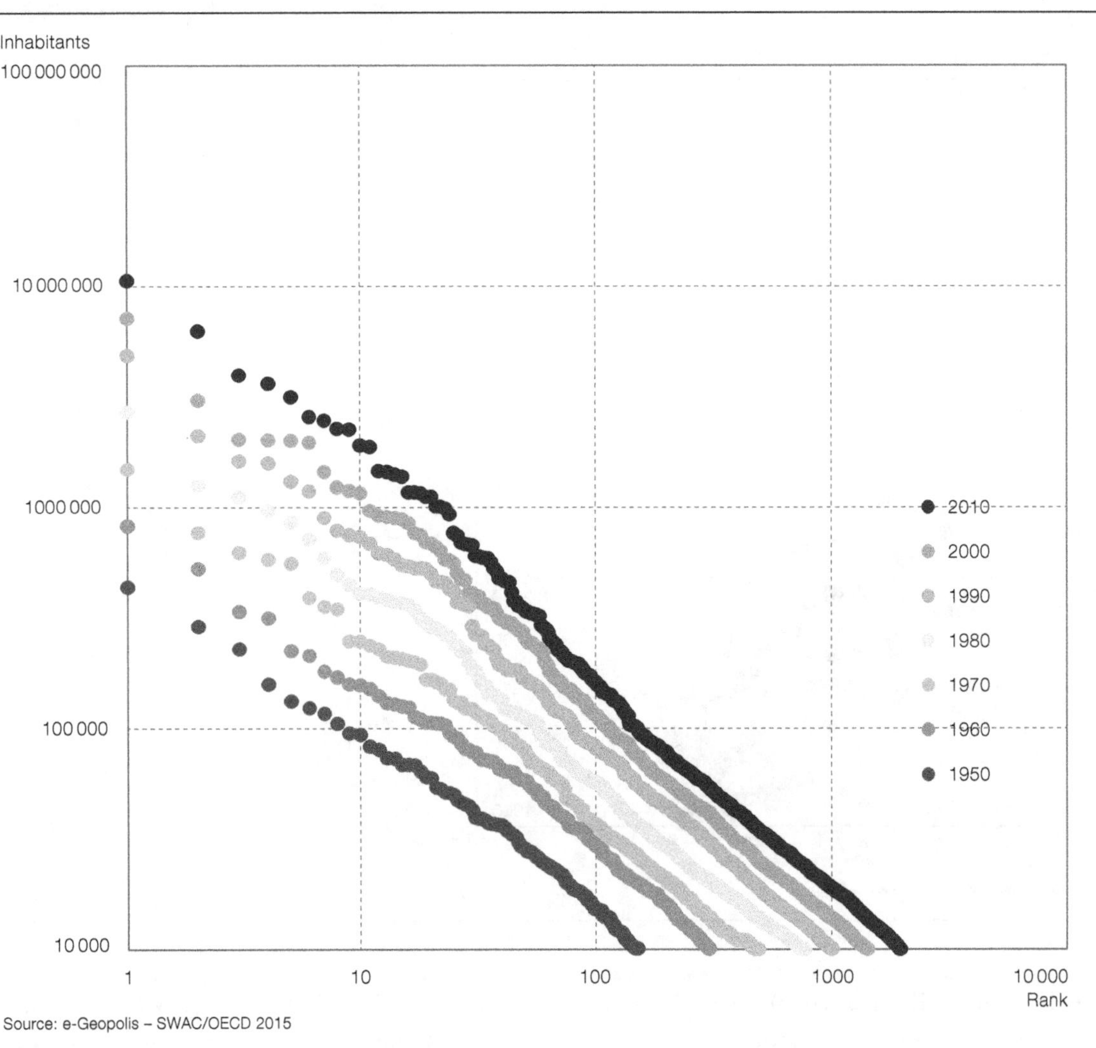

Source: e-Geopolis - SWAC/OECD 2015

2.6 A "WEST AFRICAN SYSTEM"?

The rank-size distribution of West African agglomerations

The rank-size distribution of all West African agglomerations shows an increasingly hierarchical organisation. The slope of the distribution, or the hierarchy index, increases from –0.787 in 1950 to –0.940 in 2010 (Figure 2.7 and Table 2.4). Yet it is still above –1, indicating a remaining deficit of very large agglomerations. Lagos is markedly the biggest metropolis in the region, which according to Zipf's rank-size law would lie perfectly on the regression line with 12.4 million inhabitants[3], not far from its actual 10.6 million inhabitants. However, the concavity at the top of the distribution illustrates an over-representation of large agglomerations, which corresponds to the national capitals. The urban system remains poorly integrated at a regional level (Figure 2.7).

A strong underrepresentation of medium-sized agglomerations

The idea of "integration" and "equilibrium" of a statistical distribution of cities is, however, somewhat paradoxical as it refers to a system in which the objects considered are of unequal size. In 2010, city sizes in West Africa range from 10 000 to 10.6 million inhabitants, or a ratio of 1 to 1 000. The notion of equilibrium does not relate to equality among objects, but a Pareto-Gauss distribution: according to the

Table 2.4
Linear regression parametres (least squares)

Year	Urban population (thousands)	Population of largest city (thousands)	No. of urban aggl.	Adjustment parametres	Determination coefficient
2010	132 802	10 590	1 947	y = -0.940 x + 7.094	R2 = 0.996
2000	84 512	7 178	1 417	y = -0.936 x + 6.941	R2 = 0.970
1990	56 458	4 865	1 004	y = -0.931 x + 6.794	R2 = 0.998
1980	34 733	2 690	770	y = -0.881 x + 6.515	R2 = 0.996
1970	20 181	1 487	493	y = -0.876 x + 6.333	R2 = 0.996
1960	11 977	822	305	y = -0.816 x + 6.078	R2 = 0.988
1950	5 338	436	152	y = -0.787 x + 5.764	R2 = 0.989

Source: e-Geopolis – SWAC/OECD 2015

Table 2.5
Size, class and number of agglomerations (in 2010)

Bracket	Bracket size by inhabitants	Number of agglomerations
1	10 000 to 31 622	1 384
2	31 623 to 99 999	404
3	100 000 to 316 227	93
4	316 228 to 999 999	36
5	1 000 000 à 3 162 277	18
6	3 162 278 to 9 999 999	3
7	10 000 000 to 31 622 777	1

Source: e-Geopolis – SWAC/OECD 2015

laws of Pareto, on a global level there are very few very big cities and a lot of small ones.

In order to compare population stocks according to the size of agglomerations, they need to be distributed in same frequency categories. Otherwise, the size classes will not be directly comparable. If the frequency is √10, the distribution is divided up into seven classes of which the limits would have the advantage of having rounded numbers: 10 000, 100 000, 1 million and 10 million (Table 2.5). Based on this representation, in 2010, two classes of agglomerations were over-represented: the smallest agglomerations (from 10 000 to 31 622 inhabitants), barely emerging from what is considered rural; and those from 1 to 3.16 million inhabitants, made up by half of the national capitals (Figure 2.8).

The Africapolis I study highlighted a discontinuity[4] due to a relative underrepresentation of secondary agglomerations – approximately of 100 000 to 1 million inhabitants (brackets 3 and 4). This result is confirmed by the new data (Figure 2.8). A sharp contrast emerges between the big agglomerations, situated at the interface between global and local economies, and the small towns which barely exceed 10 000 inhabitants and whose "urban" characteristics are debatable and not systematically recognised

Figure 2.8
Distribution of urban inhabitants by bracket of agglomeration size, 2010

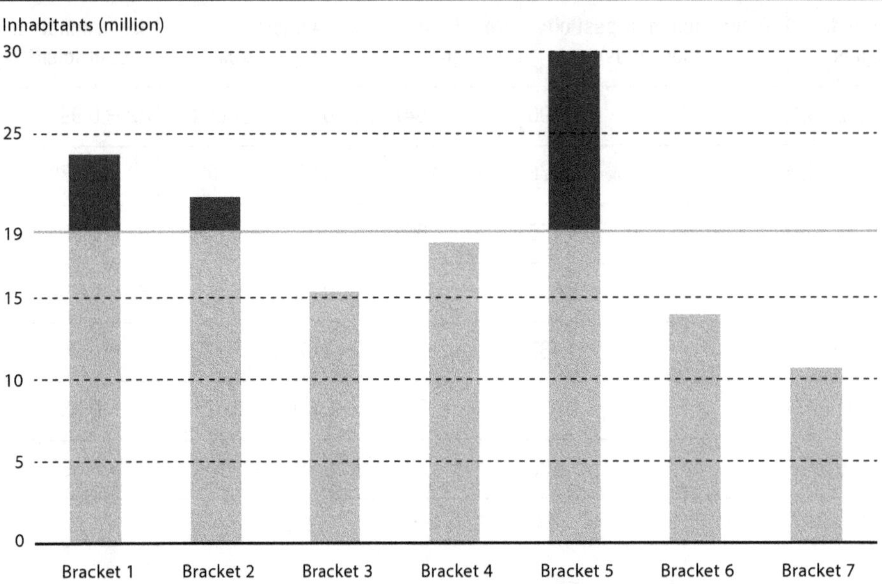

Note: See Table 2.5 for definition of the brackets.

Source: e–Geopolis - SWAC/OECD 2015

by official statistics. This dual trend emphasises the relative weakness of secondary cities.

Small agglomerations

As there are few norms concerning the size of this category of agglomerations, agglomerations of less than 100 000 are taken into account. The identification of towns of this category, which are not integrated in other international databases, is a major contribution of the e-Geopolis programme. At the bottom of the urban hierarchy, urban agglomerations continue to emerge, with 565 new agglomerations having exceeded 10 000 inhabitants since 2000.

On this basis, the population in 2010 of small- and medium-sized agglomerations (size brackets 1 and 2) was estimated at 44.8 million people, of whom half are in Nigeria (24.4 million) (Table 2.6). At the regional level, this represents 34% of the urban population. Historically, urban centres are developing by gradually being assigned administrative functions to support an increasing territorial organisation. These small- and medium-sized agglomerations continue to play a crucial role in national urban systems, representing in many countries at least one third of the urban population. In Chad, they represent 55% of the urban population.

Table 2.6

Agglomerations with 10 000 to 99 999 inhabitants in 2010

Country	Share of the urban population	Number of agglomerations	Population millions	Average size	Median size
Chad	55%	71	1.67	23 500	19 500
Benin	43%	77	1.55	20 100	15 400
Burkina Faso	43%	80	1.86	23 300	17 600
Cabo Verde	43%	3	0.10	33 300	17 100
Togo	43%	52	1.21	23 300	17 300
Niger	40%	47	1.12	23 800	17 100
Côte d'Ivoire	39%	157	3.74	23 800	18 200
Guinea	37%	34	1.17	34 400	25 900
Ghana	35%	165	3.80	23 000	16 700
Mauritania	34%	15	0.39	26 000	16 300
West Africa	34%	1 796	44.80	24 900	18 200
Nigeria	32%	930	24.41	26 400	19 400
Mali	30%	64	1.40	21 900	15 200
Gambia	28%	9	0.24	26 700	20 100
Liberia	26%	22	0.42	19 100	15 000
Sierra Leone	26%	16	0.43	26 900	17 700
Guinea Bissau	24%	5	0.14	28 000	13 400
Senegal	21%	49	1.18	24 100	17 300

Source: e-Geopolis – SWAC/OECD 2015

NOTES \\\

1 *In reality, there are 565 new agglomerations that exceeded 10 000 inhabitants, considering that 35 agglomerations were absorbed into another conurbation.*

2 *However, nine countries in West Africa share a common currency.*

3 *In the equation: y = -0,940 x + 7,094, when the x term is zero, y = 7,094, or log (12416523). 12 416 523 is the predicted population by the Zipf law, if the West African system was perfectly integrated.*

4 *The analysis of the discontinuity of urban networks relies on a rank-size model, based on Zipf's law (1949). It is used in urban geography as a descriptor of the hierarchical organisation of a system of interdependent cities within a country or region.*

Bibliography

ECOWAS/OECD (2005), *Regional Atlas of Transport and Telecommunications in the ECOWAS Zone*, Paris.

Moriconi-Ebrard, F. (1993), *L'urbanisation du monde depuis 1950*, Collection Villes, Éditions Anthropos-Economica, Paris.

Moriconi-Ebrard, F. (1996), "Explosion démographique, le sens de la démesure", *Le Monde diplomatique*, Paris, July, www.monde-diplomatique.fr/1996/07/MORICONI_EBRARD/5633.

UN-Habitat (2010), *L'état des Villes Africaines 2010: Gouvernance, inégalités, et marchés fonciers urbains*, UN-Habitat, Nairobi.

Zipf, G. K. (1941), *National Unity and Disunity, The Nation as a Bio-Social Organism*, Bloomington The Principia Press, Bloomington, Indiana.

Chapter 3

Urban morphologies and new urban forms in West Africa

The morphological processes induced by strong urban growth remain little explained and poorly measured at the micro-geographic level, except for some metropolises[1]. These processes, however, are at the core of better understanding complex urbanisation dynamics.

Firstly, the morphological processes of urban expansion reflect the forms of rural densification observed over the last 50 years as a result of population growth. Two trends are observed in West Africa:

- ancient settlement areas follow *in situ* urbanisation dynamics;
- recent settlement areas are forming large agglomerations in initially low density rural areas.

Secondly, the e-Geopolis approach allowed for the identification of different urban growth processes. They can be traced from the smallest population units (villages, neighbourhoods, localities, urban districts). They are:

- the sprawl of metropolitan regions;
- the strong expansion of secondary towns, where current road networks lead to an irregular sprawl;
- the formation of urban agglomerations from the merging of villages (for example in Benin);
- the meta-urban forms of conurbations in Nigeria.

3.1 THE DEMOGRAPHIC CONTEXT

Demographic growth, as well as national and international migration, plays a key role in explaining the evolution of city sizes and long-term *in situ* urbanisation. The observed urbanisation dynamics occurred within a context of strong demographic growth. The total population of West Africa went from 62 million inhabitants in 1950 to 323 million in 2010, an average annual growth of 2.8% over 60 years. Côte d'Ivoire, Niger, The Gambia, Togo and Senegal recorded an average annual growth rate equal to or greater than 3% between 1950 and 2010 (Table 3.1). e-Geopolis projects that the West African population will reach 490 million in 2030 and the average density will be around 150 inhabitants/km^2 in the non-desert areas of West Africa (3.3 million km^2). West Africa can then no longer be considered under-populated.

The average annual population growth rate over the last decade (2000–2010) was 3.2%, one of the highest in the world. Only Côte d'Ivoire, Cape Verde, Senegal, Guinea-Bissau and The Gambia registered a decline in their average annual growth rate relative to the preceding decade (1990–2000). Among the countries with continued very high population growth are Niger (3.9%), Burkina Faso (3.7%) and Chad (3.7%) (Table 3.1).

The impact of demographic pressure on the urbanisation process is paramount for two reasons:

- the growth of large cities is mainly driven by their natural population increase;
- the strongest urban growth occurs in the most densely populated areas.

On the one hand, the general increase in rural density as a result of demographic pressure contributes to the strong spatial expansion of secondary agglomerations; on the other hand, it forms the basis of recent urbanisation where novel and complex forms of *in situ* urbanisation are emerging (see section: forms of expansion of secondary cities). This occurs in the large settlement areas (Nigeria, Ghana, The Gambia), as well as in internal regions of the Sudano–Sahelian zone where settlement intensified (e.g. along Niger River

Table 3.1
Average annual population growth rates

	2000–10	1990–2000	1950–2010
Niger	3.9	3.4	3.3
Burkina Faso	3.7	2.6	2.9
Chad	3.7	3.6	2.8
Mali	3.6	2.6	2.5
Sierra Leone	3.5	0.8	1.9
Benin	3.5	3.2	3.0
Nigeria	3.4	3.2	2.8
West Africa	3.2	3.0	2.8
Gambia	3.2	3.2	3.1
Togo	3.0	2.8	3.0
Ghana	2.8	2.6	2.5
Guinea-Bissau	2.6	2.7	1.9
Senegal	2.4	2.7	3.0
Mauritania	2.3	2.5	2.2
Guinea	2.3	1.9	2.5
Côte d'Ivoire	2.2	3.2	3.6
Liberia	2.1	2.1	2.5
Cabo Verde	1.2	2.1	2.0

Source: e-Geopolis 2013

in Mali and in Niger with the development of irrigated agriculture).

In West Africa, the average annual growth rate of the rural population – or the non-agglomerated population, calculated by subtracting the agglomerated urban population from the total population – was 1.9% between 1950 and 2010. The rural population rose from 57 million people in 1950 to 176 million in 2010. It should continue to increase until 2030 despite a projected slowing down of the growth rate. One quarter of the new rural population will be in Nigeria.

Map 3.1
Estimated rural densities in West Africa

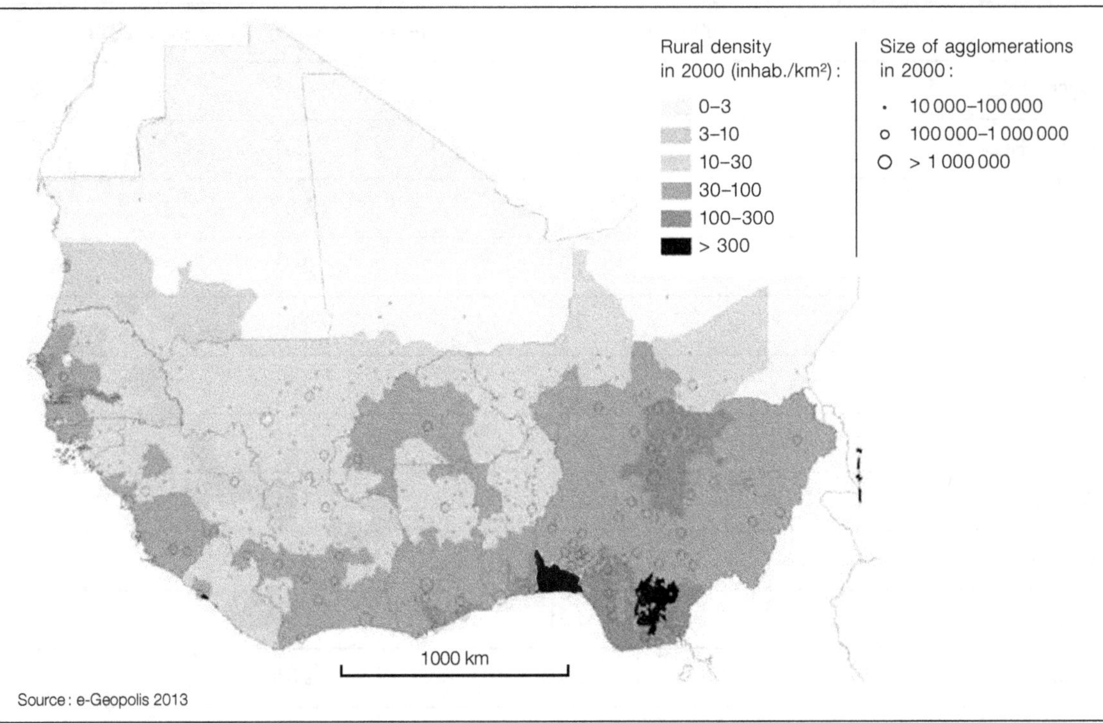

Source: e-Geopolis 2013

3.2 TOWARDS THE FORMATION OF METROPOLITAN REGIONS

The size of metropolises and the primacy index do not always capture the real role of some metropolitan areas in the urbanisation process. In Liberia, Guinea, Burkina Faso, Chad, Niger and Mauritania, a metropolis is an agglomeration surrounded by sparsely populated rural sectors. In Mauritania and Niger, Nouakchott and Niamey expand in desert areas. In the other countries, however, metropolises spread out to dense peripheries and in some cases satellite agglomerations. Conurbations are forming through a combination of absorption of peripheral localities and strong urban infill[2]. This is the case in Senegal, Benin, Côte d'Ivoire, Mali, The Gambia and Nigeria (Table 3.2).

In some developed countries, the definition of "metropolitan areas" (United States) or "urban areas" (France) allows to capture such ensembles, encompassing the city centre, outskirts and peri-urban areas. This definition does not yet exist in Africa due to a lack of statistical data. Indeed, a metropolitan area is defined based on flows, but there are no statistics on mobility.

"Satellite" agglomerations are often too small to drastically change the size of metropolises (in Abidjan and Lagos, their population barely adds 5% to the main agglomeration). However, in some countries, the spatial sprawling process[3] creates an urbanisation by "leaps". The process of absorption[4] and merging[5] with other agglomerations can rapidly increase the size of metropolises and even the level of urbanisation. This has been observed in the densely populated areas of East and Central Africa. In West Africa, Nigeria, Ghana and Benin are countries that have particularly experienced this process.

In Ghana, the Accra agglomeration has already merged with Tema New-Town whose population was estimated at 40 000 inhabitants in 1990. Accra continues to project north along the Kumasi route in the linear shaped and still distinct agglomerations (Aburi, Akropong), but which will soon be absorbed (Map 3.2).

In Benin, Cotonou and Porto Novo (the second largest agglomeration in the country and 15 km away) could merge[6]. The morphological link is supported by the agglomerations of

Table 3.2
Overview of the spatial expansion of metropolitan regions

	Composition of metropolitan regions in the formation process
Senegal	Dakar, Bargny, + three small agglomerations towards Thiès + linear development along the route towards Yenne Guedji and Mbour. The expansion of the Dakar agglomeration exceeding its limits to the north and south should be considered, within the development context as the Dakar-Touba « development corridor », one of the more striking examples of how West African urban networks are becoming linear.
Benin	Cotonou and Porto Novo. The morphological link between these two agglomerations is due to two small agglomerations, Ekpé and Djeregbé (Map 3.2)
Côte d'Ivoire	Abidjan/Bingerville + Grand Bassam. The most recent satellite images shows urban sprawl between these two agglomerations.
Mali	Bamako, Kati, Baguineda, Diatoula. The northern borders of Bamako are not clear due to great urban sprawl; the Kati agglomeration that extends to the east is a dispersed settlement area.
Gambia	Serrekunda, Brikama, Gunjur, Tanjeh, Kunkujang. The case in The Gambia is similar although less than the complex conurbations in Nigeria. New localities are popping up and being directly absorbed into existing agglomerations.
Nigeria	Lagos, Ikorodu, Loburo, Agbarra, Magbon, Igbesa

Source: e-Geopolis – SWAC/OECD 2015

Map 3.2
Urban agglomerations around Accra, Ghana and in southern Benin in 2010

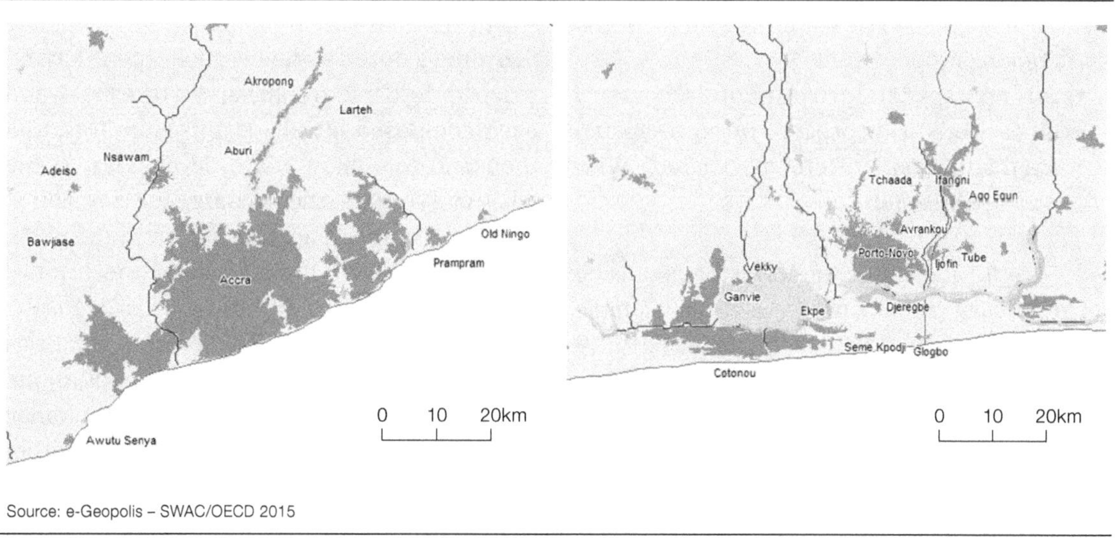

Source: e-Geopolis – SWAC/OECD 2015

Ekpé (45 000 inhabitants in 2010) and Djeregbe (11 000 inhabitants). The metropolitan region will extend beyond Porto Novo and, with the absorption of Avrankrou, Tchaada and Ifanngi, it would form a region with more than 2.5 million inhabitants by 2030 (Map 3.2).

Similar phenomena are not limited to the big metropolises (Burgel et al, 1995) and are observed in smaller urban areas such as Bohicon-Abomey in Benin and Kumasi in Ghana.

3.3 SPATIAL EXPANSION OF SECONDARY CITIES

Plates 3.1 and 3.2 show how urban sprawl is never uniformly distributed around the periphery of a large city. Cities are constrained by obstacles (water bodies, slopes) and spread across different areas (agricultural land, forests, villages, etc.). These obstacles impact significantly on the form of cities, as well as on their institutional and economic aspects:

- by absorption of villages, hamlets and peripheral gaps;
- by private and/or public urban development programmes with new neighbourhoods located far from centres;
- by unregulated development, which leads to substantial urban sprawl into "empty" and agricultural areas on the periphery. In the Sahelian and Saharan areas where the terrain poses few physical constraints, spatial expansion can be at times spectacular.

As cities expand, differences (settlement, construction and economy) seem to continue, if not intensify, raising two issues:

- Rural-type housing dominating many peripheral areas where economic activity still involves a certain level of agricultural activity, even within the limits of the agglomeration.
- Strong spatial growth of secondary cities leads to a process of socio-spatial fragmentation, often associated with metropolitisation.

Plate 3.1 illustrates the forms of expansion of secondary cities using Kayes as an example, an agglomeration of 142 000 inhabitants in 2010, located in the north west of Mali. Satellite images highlight the agglomeration's three physical expansion "patterns" between 2003 and 2011.

The merging of "villages"

Growth of existing localities (large villages, villages, hamlets) to exceed 10 000 inhabitants explains the emergence of most new urban agglomerations. However, the increased interconnection among settlements has led to changes in the process of expansion. The intensification of flows and mobility translates into a 'linearisation' of urban networks. Villages and small localities expand towards each other along infrastructure networks and are merging to form one single urban agglomeration.

The merging of villages remains a modest phenomenon in relation to the number and size of the agglomerations concerned. In 2010, a few hundred agglomerations with less than 50 000 inhabitants were identified and measured in Benin, Burkina Faso, Côte d'Ivoire, Ghana, The Gambia, Liberia, Mali, Senegal, Sierra Leone and Togo. These agglomerations were made up of two or more local units classified as rural (villages, settlements and localities). Half of them are located in Benin and Ghana, where linear settlements are most prominent. This merging contributes to the recomposition of local territories and their economies. Nioro in Mali is an urban agglomerations made up of several villages that emerged in an agricultural perimetre. Similarly, the shores of Lake Ahémé in Benin are in the process of complete merging: a dozen agglomerations, none having reached the demographic urban threshold, and each composed of villages of a hundred to a thousand inhabitants, are developing on the basis of a dense settlement area.

The Akropong agglomeration in the north of Accra spreads linearly along the Kumasi route over close to 20 km long. In 2010, the agglomeration, made up of nine localities with between 2 300 to 11 000 inhabitations, reached 46 000 inhabitants. This agglomeration, separated from the capital by another "road" agglomeration (Aburi) can be seen as a spatial projection of Accra. The linearisation of the urban network continues north towards Ho with two more agglomerations that are forming along the road.

Plate 3.1
Spatial growth patterns in Kayes (Mali): 16 February 2003 vs. 27 October 2011

a. Planned development – subdivision

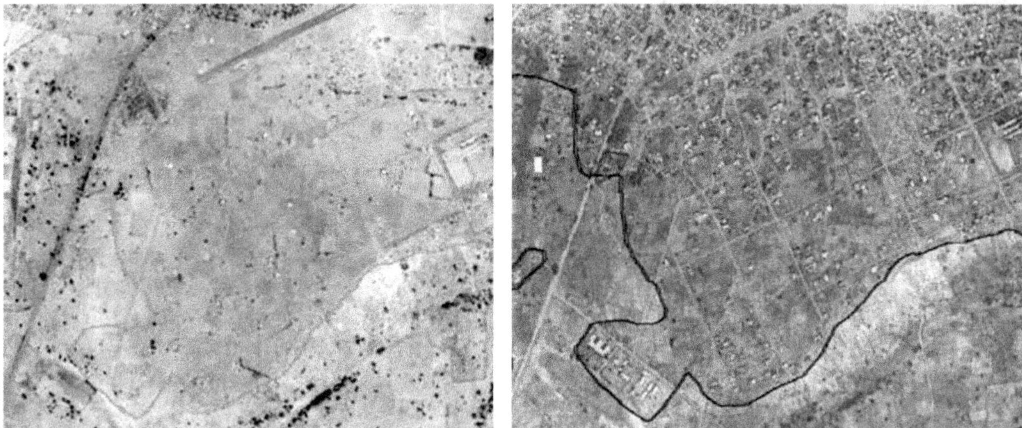

b. Unplanned development – sprawl, urban-type housing

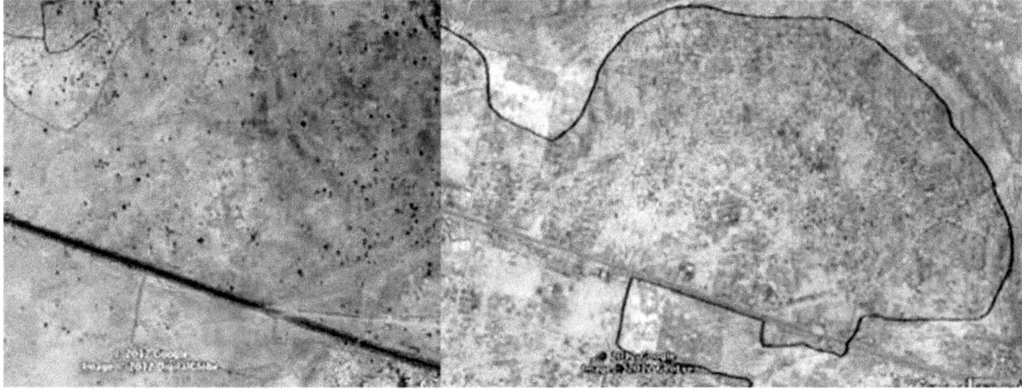

c. Merging of villages and peripheral gaps – rural type housing

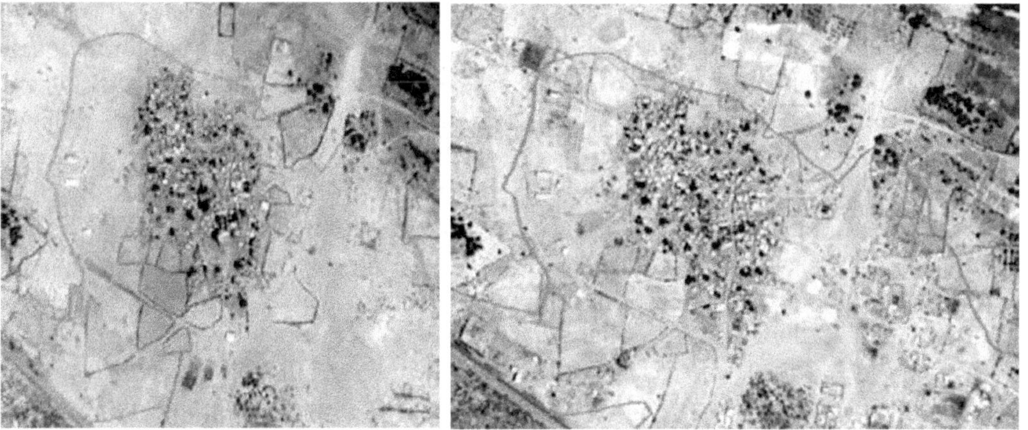

Sources: Google Earth (2012), Kayes, Mali, Available at http://www.google.com/earth/download/ge/agree.html (Viewed 29 November 2012)

Plate 3.2
Urban area of the Akropong agglomeration, Ghana

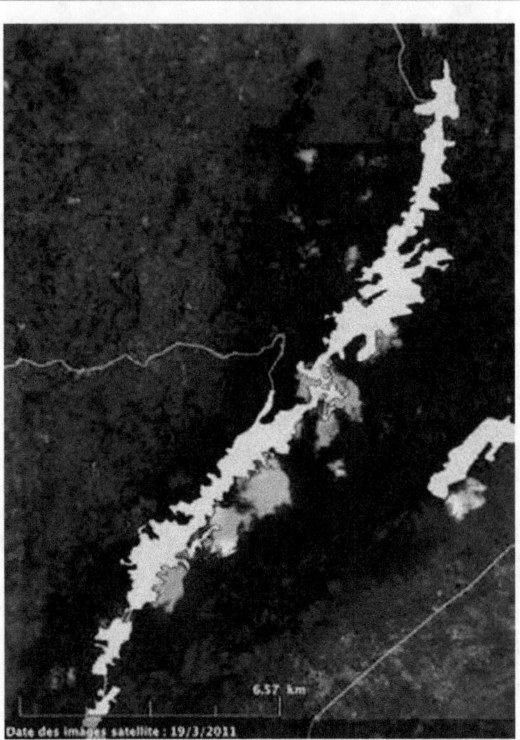

Sources: Google Earth (2012), Akropong, Ghana, Available at http://www.google.com/earth/download/ge/agree.html (Viewed 29 November 2012)

Notes: *Google Earth image and e-Geopolis urban area*

Nigeria's conurbations: From hyper rural to meta-urban

Most Nigerian conurbations formed at the end of the 1990s as a result of the densification of scattered settlements in the densely populated areas of the Niger Delta. The demographic density of the Imo and Anambra states to the east of the river, and the Local Government Areas (LGAs) of the neighbouring Aba, Rivers, Akwa Ibom states, reached 1 000 inhabitants per km^2 in 2010. Among the conurbations identified, four had more than 1 million inhabitants in 2010 (Table 3.3). In 1990 Onitsha was an urban agglomeration of 620 000 inhabitants. By 2010 it had grown to become the second largest agglomeration in Nigeria with 6.28 million inhabitants after it merged with around twenty agglomerations that each had 10 000 or more inhabitants in 1990. More spread out than Lagos, it covers close to 2 000 km^2, but is far less dense (3 200 inhab/km^2) (Plate 3.3).

The territorial development processes underway, observed on several levels (metropolises, secondary agglomerations, merging of villages and conurbations), share a common key characteristic: the densification of settlement areas that leads to "scattered urbanisation" of areas that were previously considered rural. Conurbations and agglomerations, created as a result of merging villages, are pushing the frontier of what is urban. Hence, the criteria that distinguish urban from rural are being re-examined one by one: densities, type of housing and the importance of agriculture. These agglomerations are less dense than large cities but much denser than rural areas: from 2 300 to 2 600 inhabitants per km^2 in Uyo, Nsukka and Aba and 3 300 inhabitants per km^2 in Akropong and Onitsha. The lower levels of the urban hierarchy still need to be examined.

Urbanisation in Africa is part of the very current and universal processes: infill, development on the outskirts of metropolises and secondary cities, inclusion of agricultural zones within the geographic limits of urban agglomerations and the merging of agglomerations at various sizes.

Plate 3.3

Urban imprint of the Onitsha conurbation, Nigeria in 2011

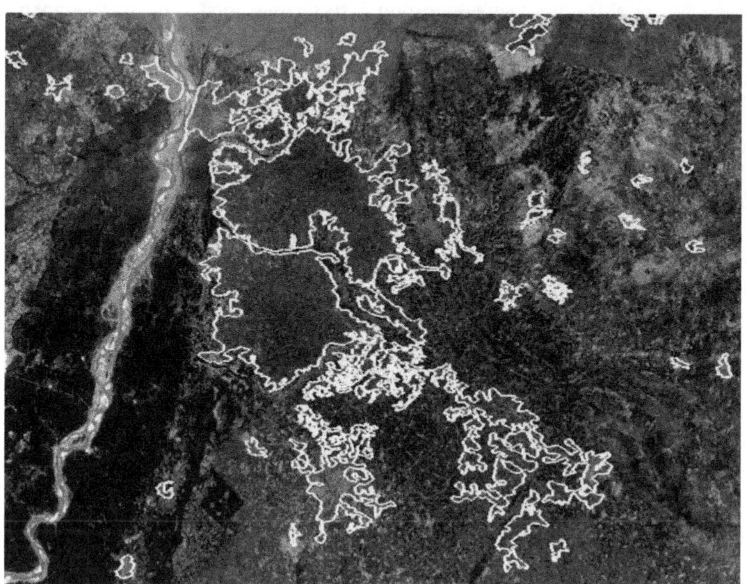

Sources: Google Earth (2012), Onitsha, Nigeria, Available at http://www.google.com/earth/download/ge/agree.html (Viewed 29 November 2012)

Notes : Google Earth image and e-Geopolis urban area

Table 3.3

The main urban conurbations in Nigeria in 2010

	Population 2010 (millions)	Surface area (km²)	Density (inhab/km²)
Onitsha	6.28	1 965	3 196
Uyo	1.88	729	2 579
Nsukka	1.46	645	2 264
Aba	1.01	384	2 630

Source: e-Geopolis – SWAC/OECD 2015

Table 3.4
Composition of the Onitsha conurbation: Population of absorbed agglomerations

Name	State	LGA	Population 1990	Population 2000	Population 2010
Onitsha	**Anambra**	**Onitsha North**	**620 000**	**1 450 000**	**6 280 000**
Umuahia	Imo	Umuahia North	120 000	0	0
Awka	Anambra	Awka South	90 000	0	0
Nkwerre	Imo	Nkwerre	90 000	0	0
Orlu	Imo	Orlu	75 000	0	0
Oguta	Imo	Oguta	25 000	0	0
Okporo	Imo	Oru East	20 000	0	0
Nibo	Anambra	Awka South	15 000	0	0
Nnewi	Anambra	Nnewi North	160 000	300 000	0
Ihiala	Anambra	Ihiala	70 000	180 000	0
Urualla	Imo	Ideato North	110 000	150 000	0
Enugu Ukwu Uruogbo	Anambra	Njikoka	50 000	90 000	0
Amauzari Okwosu	Imo	Isiala Mbano	50 000	90 000	0
Uli	Imo	Ihiala	35 000	45 000	0
Ozubolu	Anambra	Nnewi North	30 000	42 000	0
Nkume	Imo	Njaba	20 000	40 000	0
Mgbidi	Imo	Oru West	20 000	30 000	0
Amaraka	Imo	Isiala Mbano	11 000	20 000	0
		Absorbed population	**435 000**	**987 000**	

Note: "0" indicates that the population of the agglomeration was absorbed.
Source: e-Geopolis – SWAC/OECD 2015

NOTES \\

1 *The State of African Cities 2010, United Nations Human Settlements Programme (UN-HABITAT).*

2 *Infill: The process whereby the average distance between single structures (isolated constructions) becomes less than 200 metres and the total population exceeds 10 000 inhabitants.*

3 *Sprawl: The built-up area of an agglomeration spreads to land which has not yet been built upon.*

4 *Absorption: The built-up area of an urban agglomeration joins up that of villages and hamlets or isolated buildings which are henceforth included in the agglomeration.*

5 *Merging (coalescence): The built-up area of villages and hamlets, initially distinct and separate, merge. The sum of their populations exceeds 10 000 inhabitants, thus forming a new agglomeration.*

6 *The development and function of this urban region was studied in the 2000s by E. Dorier-Apprill and E. Domingo (2004).*

Bibliography

Burgel, G. et al (dir.) (1995), "Villes secondaires d'Afrique", *Villes en parallèle*, No. 22, pp. 17–36, December.

Dorier-Apprill, E. and E. Domingo (2004), "Les nouvelles échelles de l'urbain en Afrique : Métropolisation et nouvelles dynamiques territoriales sur le littoral béninois", *Vingtième Siècle*, No. 81, Presses de Sciences Po, Paris, pp. 41–54, http://dx.doi.org/10.3917/ving.081.0041.

Chapter 4

Estimating the population of Nigerian cities

A more detailed analysis of Nigeria is provided due to its demographic importance, controversies over official population data and the lack of data at the local level. These problems require specific methodologies to estimate the population of each agglomeration and to calculate urban indicators. A critical review of the census and mapping sources, as well as a description of the assumptions and their consequences, are proposed. The obtained data is then tested (distribution, hierarchy, etc.), and compared and confronted with theoretical models[7].

Generally, projections of urban growth are based on models developed in urban geography or spatial economics. These data do not aim to estimate population by city, but rather a total at the national level. A hypothetico-deductive approach consists of testing the theoretically-derived results with the empirical reality. However, in Nigeria's case local empirical data is flawed and the results from statistical sources are unverifiable. Thus this top-down approach quickly reaches its limits.

While the theoretical models are able to produce results that are relatively consistent at the national level, they cannot reproduce local diversity. Yet not all populations of urban agglomerations have access to the urban services of a large city. They do not have the same resource endowments, do not benefit in the same way from access to roads and highways, nor are they organised according to an identical economic and social system.

As a result, the e-Geopolis team applied an inductive methodology. This is based on following a bottom-up approach, going from a small subject, in his case a group of houses, and working one's way up to the national level through the aggregation of successive results. The same approach was used in the first version of Africapolis I. However, the new results question some of the conclusions reached in the preceding study. These new results were obtained through better availability and higher quality satellite data and a more prudent use of sources – notably a critical analysis of the Local Government Area (LGA) data and corrections to the 2011 official estimate.

4.1 THE ISSUE

A unique example of urbanisation in Africa

Although census figures have been disputed for the past fifty years, it is clear that Nigeria is and will continue to be for a very long time the most populated country on the African continent. The size of its market dwarfs that of its immediate neighbours, which are eight to seventeen times less populated – Cameroon, Niger, Chad and Benin. Today half of West Africa's population lives in Nigeria.

The country's urban characteristics are equally exceptional. As the world's 5th largest oil exporter, the country has invested heavily in its road infrastructure. Besides South Africa, no other country on the continent has a similarly extended and dense road network. Its highway and paved road network contrast with the state of its neighbours' road network. This dense infrastructure network promotes urban development.

Based on a diversified manufacturing sector (agro-food, chemicals, steel, cement, textiles), Nigerian industries have been exporting their products for decades to all African countries. Maps and images confirm the existence of large industrial areas, veritable modern industrial zones, in several cities. The existence of large industrial areas has been a historical factor of urbanisation across the world (Bairoch, 1985). The service sector, including banking, insurance and trade, is very developed, providing employment in big urban centres. The country's

Table 4.1

Total population of Nigeria, official and corrected data

Total population (thousands)	1952	1952–53	1962	1963	1991	2006	2011
Official	30 400	31 050	45 332	55 670	88 992	140 432	167 913
Corrected		33 160	41 055	42 000			
Notes	1		2	3	4	5	6

[1] Official: 1952 Population Census, 30.4 million + 650 000 inhabitants of Northern Cameroons (rattaché in 1961 and counted in 1953). Corrected: based on the USCB estimate.

[2] Official: Preliminary counting in 1962 carried out in preparation of the 1963 census. Corrected: based on an annual growth rate of 2.3% per year between 1952 and 1962.

[3] Official: 1963 Population census. Corrected: based on the annual growth rate of 2.3% between 1962 and 1963.

[4] Population census of 26 November 1991

[5] Population census of 21 March 2006

[6] Headcount: Estimate communicated by the Nigerian Census Bureau (October 2011)

Source: e-Geopolis 2013

maritime ports serve the large domestic market as well as its landlocked neighbours to the north, Niger and Chad.

In addition, Nigeria has a particular ethnological context, with the presence of several communities on its territory at the origin of ancient urban settlements. In the southwest, the urban Yoruba people (Oyo Kingdom) have a dense network of cities of which twenty exceeded 20000 inhabitants by the end of the 19th century. Besides the settlements in the southwest, accounting for a fifth of the population, are the Hausa people in the north. The Hausa settlements are organised around centuries-old cities that were the main hubs between West Africa and the Holy Land of Islam. As early as the 11th century, religion and trade were already developing. While the Hausa population is about the same size as that of the Yoruba, each approximately 20% of the national population (Mustapha, 2006), their presence throughout the rest of the country and beyond (Niger, Cameroon, Sudan and Ghana) promoted the establishment of continent-wide trade networks. Even prior to British colonisation, northern cities such as Kano, Maiduguri, Sokoto, Zaria, Bida and Yola had over 10000 inhabitants. The Niger Delta, with demographic density comparable to that of the Indo-Gangetic Plain of Asia, has traditionally been agricultural, yet the river and its numerous streams have encouraged the development of trade. Urban centres such as Aba, Calabar, Onitsha, Port Harcourt developed and exceeded 10000 inhabitants as early the 1920s. As from the 1911 census, e-Geopolis has identified 50 cities exceeding 10000 inhabitants. Despite statistics either lacking or being of questionable quality, Nigeria's high urbanisation level compared to that in the rest of West Africa is more than an assumption.

4.2 LACK OF RELIABLE DEMOGRAPHIC DATA

As in most countries where national political representation and a rentier state's distribution of wealth depends on the demographic weight of regions, and where these coincide with ethno linguistic or religious groups, censuses entail political, material and symbolic stakes.

National censuses

Problems appeared as early as the 1963 census. The 55.7 million inhabitants enumerated in 1963 imply an annual growth rate of 5.4% since the preceding census of 1952 (31.1 million) (Table 4.1). One of the explanations put forward is that the 1952 census has suffered from important omissions. Although this hypothesis cannot be excluded, it seems insufficient. A careful analysis of the 1963 figures shows a systematic over-representation of the 20–39 year old male population (Figure 4.1). While such cases are routinely recorded, in particular in Africa's mining or industrial towns that attract male

Figure 4.1
Age distribution bias in 1963 Nigerian census data and correction by second degree polynomial regression

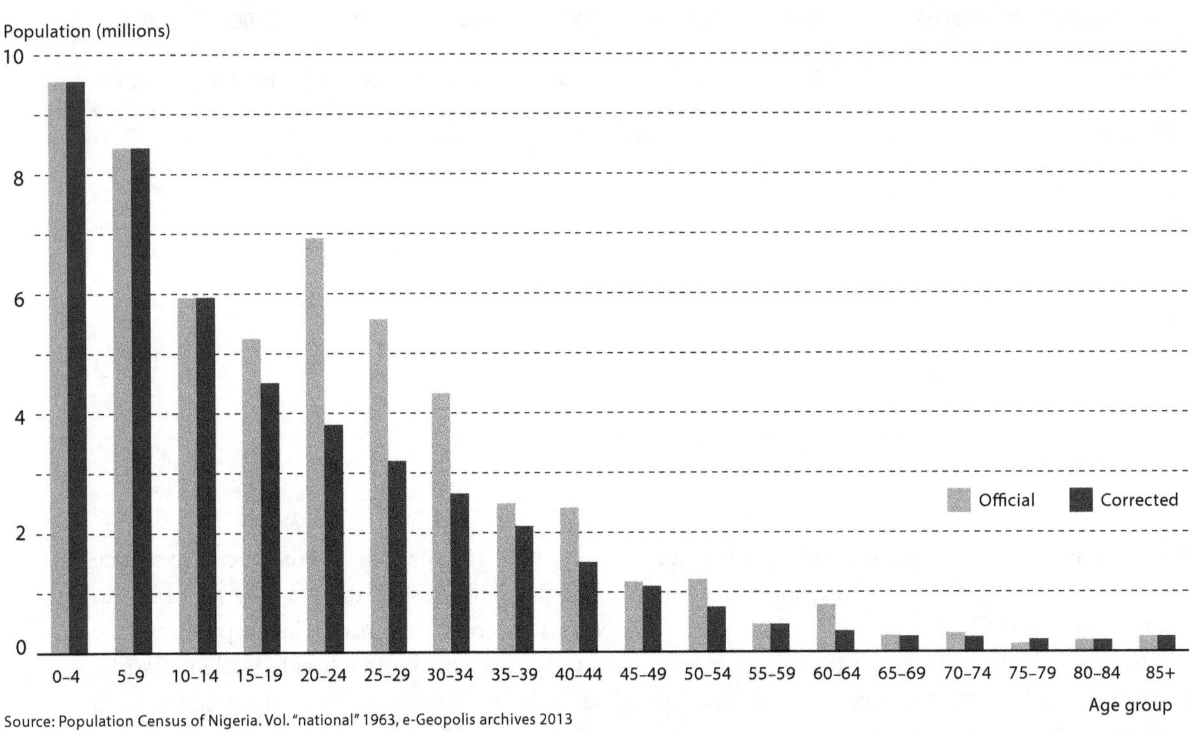

Source: Population Census of Nigeria. Vol. "national" 1963, e-Geopolis archives 2013

workers who, through remittances, provide resources to the rest of the family in their home region, such a scenario is not possible at the level of an entire country. While this manipulation is obvious in Figure 4.1, it is difficult however to smooth out the distribution due to a lack of detailed data. As the civil register is incomplete and the age of individuals uncertain, the age distribution suffered from an "attractiveness of round numbers" bias. That is, many adults know that they are about 40, 50 or 60 years of age and declare rather a rounded number than their actual age leading to and inflation of age brackets ending with "0". There is little doubt that inhabitants, or statistical services under political pressure, or a combination of the two, add phantom inhabitants. This can be caused by wanting a certain group to appear more influential. For this reason, young working men are added rather than women, children or old people. Only the 20–24, 25–29 and 30–34 age groups show an estimated seven million person surplus. The question to ask is then, does the addition concern *only* young men?

An alternative method of estimating the population of Nigeria at that time consists of using the results from a preparatory operation to establish the geographic subdivisions to be counted during the 1962 census and which reported 45.3 million inhabitants (Table 4.1). The results of the 1962 pre-census are also the basis for the United Nations Statistical Services during the 1970s. Assuming a growth rate of 2.3%, the population would have increased by about one million inhabitants between 1962 and 1963. The UN demographic register gives a population of 46.3 million inhabitants in 1963.

However, even using the 1962 estimate (45.3 million), the annual growth rate between 1952 and 1962 would still be too high (4%). It is worth noting that between the two censuses, Nigeria grew by 46 700 km^2 and around 650 000 inhabitants (in 1953) by annexing the former part of British Cameroon called *Northern Cameroons*[2] in 1961 (Map 4.1). Adding the population of *Northern Cameroons* to the population of Nigeria in 1952 brings the Nigeria's total population in 1952 up to 31.1 million, and the annual growth rate down to 3.8%. Yet, it is widely accepted that it could hardly exceed 2.3% at that time (the infant mortality rate was estimated at 189 per thousand at the beginning

Map 4.1

Nigerian territory after the annexation of British Cameroon in 1961

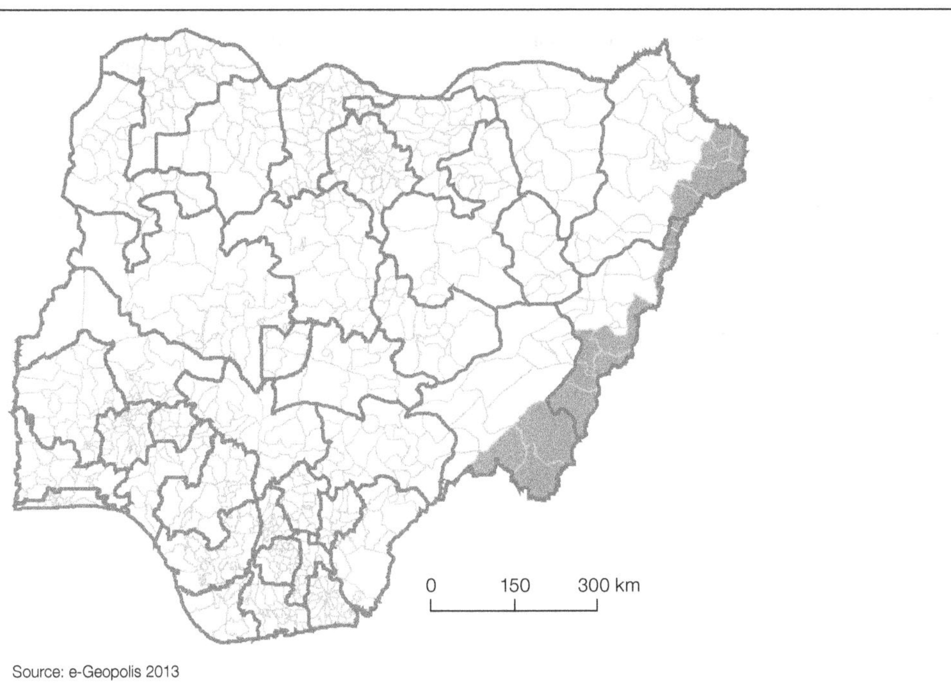

Source: e-Geopolis 2013

of the 1950s and a mortality rate of 27.7 per thousand compared with 15.1 per thousand today). At that growth rate (2.3%) Nigeria would have only counted 41 million inhabitants in 1962. It therefore seems clear that not *only* young men were added.

How can we explain this? One possible explanation is the 1960s Biafran war, which exacerbated competition between regions and groups. A new census was carried out in 1973, enumerating 79.8 million inhabitants, but the results were officially annulled. The 1991 census then counted 89 million inhabitants. With respect to the 45.3 inhabitants counted in the 1962 pre-census, this implies an average annual population increase of 2.4%. However, in terms of population growth, this was a very heterogeneous period. The Biafran war and ensuing famine at the end of the 1960s may have cost between two to four million lives, equal to two to four years of natural population increase.

Finally, the March 2006 census enumerates 140.4 million inhabitants, implying an average growth rate of 3.1% since 1991. Initially, this increase seems exaggerated, and even more so the annual growth rate of 3.6% between 2006 and the 167.9 million officially estimated in 2011. Thus in the 2008 Africapolis report, it was assumed that the population of Nigeria was, again, over-estimated at the end of the observed period.

A new element has fed the debate since 2008. The publication of the first results of the censuses carried out in Benin, Niger, Mauritania and Mali show a slight rebound in natural population growth since 2000, challenging the view that demographic growth in West Africa was permanently on the decline.

It is assumed, however, that this increase in the population growth rate is a temporary fluctuation arising from the demographic transition. As such, it would not be caused by a rise in the birth rate, but rather a strong decline in the mortality rate and more precisely in infant mortality. This decline in the mortality rate could be one of the results of improved access to health services and thus an indirect effect of the densification of the network of small towns.

In addition, the beginning of the 2000s was a prosperous period for the Nigerian economy, with GDP increasing by more than 5% annually. This positive environment could have attracted stronger migration flows from neighbouring countries, in particular Niger and Chad. However, neither of these two hypotheses can be verified by available statistics.

Table 4.2
The results of the last four censuses in West Africa

	Census date and results				Annual average growth rate between censuses		
Benin	1 Apr 1979 3 331 210	15 Feb 1992 4 915 555	15 Feb 2002 6 769 914	11 May 2013 9 983 884	3.1	3.3	3.5
Mali	16 Dec 1976 6 394 918	1 Apr 1987 7 696 348	1 Apr 1998 9 810 912	1 Apr 2009 14 517 176	1.8	2.2	3.6
Niger	20 Nov 1977 5 102 990	10 May 1988 7 251 626	20 May 2001 11 060 291	10 Dec 2012 17 129 076	3.4	3.3	3.8
Mauritania	1 Jan 1977 1 338 830	5 Apr 1998 1 865 236	1 Nov 2000 2 508 159	25 Mar 2013 3 387 868	3.0	2.4	2.5

Source: Compilation of census data, e-Geopolis archives 2013

Table 4.3
Scenario of the evolution of the total population

	1950	1960	1970	1980	1990	2000	2010
Total population (thousands)	31 800	39 230	49 300	65 700	86 950	119 350	166 164

	1950–60	1960–70	1970–80	1980–90	1990–00	2000–10
Average growth rate	2.1%	2.3%	2.9%	2.8%	3.2%	3.4%

Source: e-Geopolis 2013

Contrary to the 2008 Africapolis report, it was decided that the figures in the 1991 and 2006 censuses were to be considered reliable. Given Nigeria's size, these changes however also have significant repercussions on the size of the regional population of West Africa as well as on demographic projections.

The debate is not over, and Nigeria's demographic dynamics should be interpreted with caution.

The revisions adopted in Africapolis

Our estimates of Nigeria's total population is based on several sources prior to 1970, and then uses official data for 1990 onwards, as the results of the 1991 and 2006 censuses and the 2011 estimates are considered reliable at the national level. The figures for 1950 and 1960 are interpolated based on the corrected data from 1952 and 1962. The figures for 1970 and 1980 interpolated based on the 1962 corrected data and 1991 census results. The results are significantly below the data published in international publications (UN, World Bank, etc.) (Table 1.5). Using this approach, the proposed scenario of the evolution of Nigeria's total population is presented in Table 4.3.

The correction applied to urban populations

How can the urban population in this country be evaluated within this context? e-Geopolis systematically takes data by gender and age group from the 1963 census publications and

Figure 4.2
Distribution of the Ilorin UC population by age group in 1963

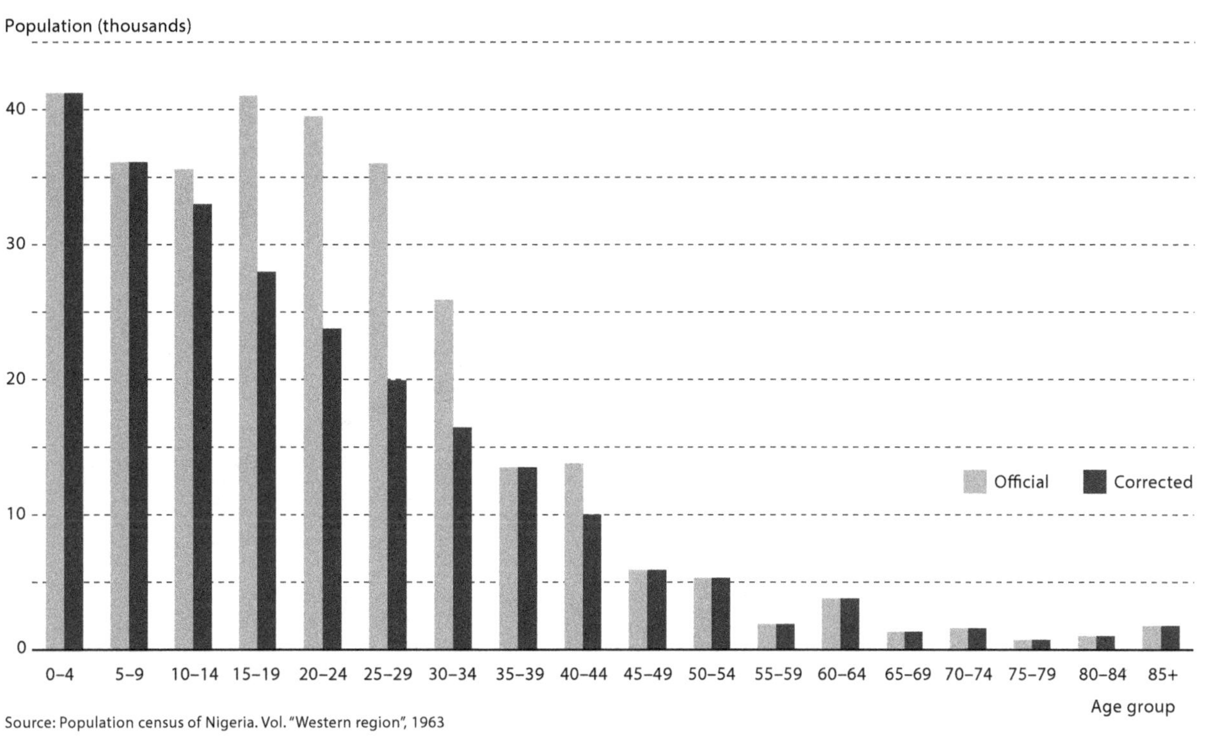

Source: Population census of Nigeria. Vol. "Western region", 1963

corrects the population figures city by city. The 1963 data is unfortunately not broken down by locality, and only available for geographic subdivisions classified as *"District council"* (DC), *"Local council"* (LC), *"Urban council"* (UC), and *"Group"* (G). In the census publications, the territorial divisions are then regrouped by *Census District*, then by *Division and Province* and published in five regional volumes (machine typed and containing apparently several typing errors).

Figure 4.2 offers an example of the distribution by age group for the Ilorin *Urban council* in 1963. The total population is 305 900 inhabitants. After smoothing the data to remove any over-representation, there are 245 200 inhabitants left. The same deflation rate applied to the city of Ilorin results in 171 600 inhabitants, down from 208 600 inhabitants. An estimate based on the 1962 pre-census gives 179 100 inhabitants. This difference, between the smoothing applied figure (171 600) and the 1962 based estimate (179 100), could be due to an actual over-representation of working-age males in Ilorin, as observed in most large African cities. This actual over-representation of working-age males, however, is certainly less than that expressed in the official figures

The dataset corrected by the 1962 pre-census probably provides the best results. Although at the national level the results between the two correction approaches are relatively similar, there are important regional differences. The data correction therefore raises the problem of how over-counting affected different regions and different cities. The correction at subnational level is thereby complicated. In other words, the problems related to the population censuses are coupled with problems related to administrative subdivisions and cartography.

Figure 4.3
Rank-size distribution of localities with more than 6 500 inhabitants in the former State of Sokoto in 1963 (logarithmic scale)

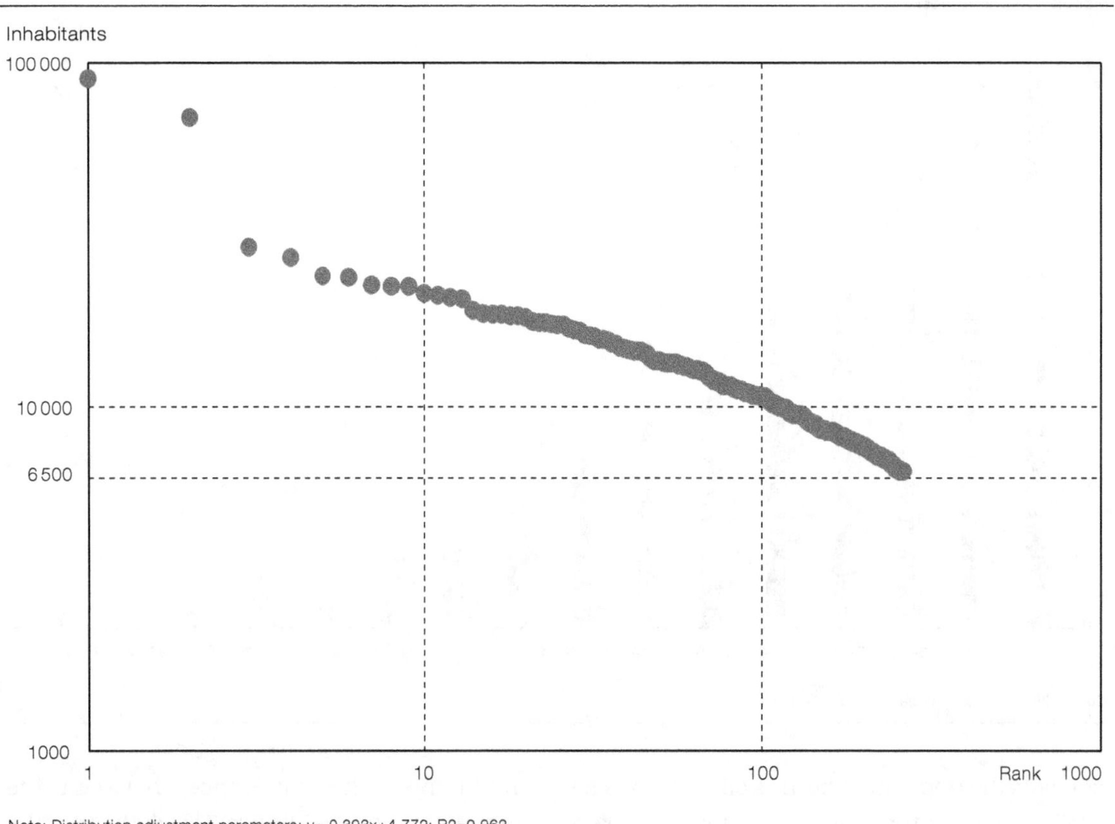

Note: Distribution adjustment parameters: y=-0,393x+4,772; R2=0,962.
Source: Population census of Nigeria 1963, Vol. Northern, e-Geopolis archives 2013

4.3 THE PARTICULARITIES OF GEOGRAPHIC SUBDIVISIONS IN NIGERIA

After 1963, census results were not published at a geographic level lower than that of the "Local Government Areas" (LGAs) (774 in the 2006 census). While neighbouring French-speaking countries publish *village registries*, Ghana and The Gambia publish *gazetteers* of localities as of 1931; Nigeria has not published any such type of inventory over the past 50 years. No official list of cities and villages is available for Nigeria.

The list of localities published in 1963 corresponded to administrative entities of which the boundaries are not known, and for the most part are not mapped. In addition, the cartography of the administrative network of the 774 LGAs suffers from so many inconsistencies that its cross-referencing with other source – aerial photography, satellite image or GPS data – does not allow for any verification of the terrain.

The special case of "localities"

It is worth further examining the 1963 concept of *"locality"* given the absence of maps or any explanatory document; it is also worth assessing the constraints to their mapping, as this provides an essential source for estimating the population of agglomerations.

The Nigerian locality of 1963 does not define a small town or a village with its surrounding areas, but rather a rural territory of which the perimetre is unknown. In the State of Sokoto, the population officially reached 4.33 million in 1963. According to detailed data, there were approximately 100 localities of more than 10 000 inhabitants, accounting for 36% of the state's total population, and 227 localities with more than 6 500 inhabitant. In Sokoto, 80% of the population lived in localities of more than

Figure 4.4
Model of administrative divisions in English-speaking West African countries

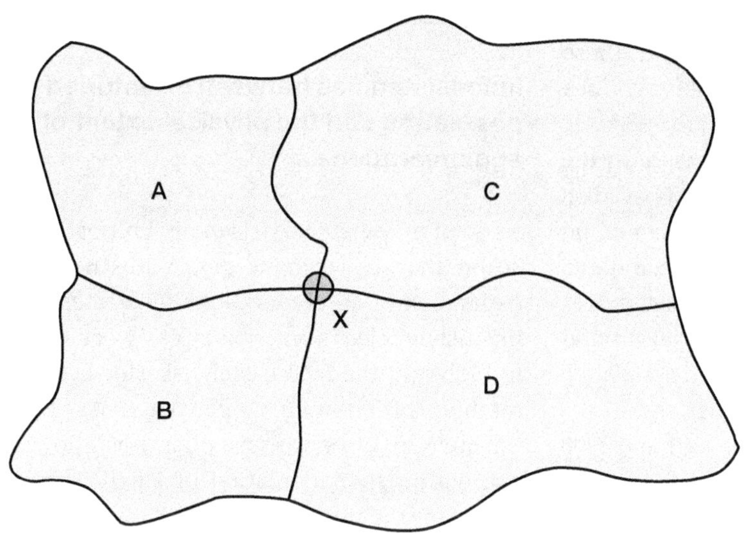

Source: e-Geopolis – SWAC/OECD 2015

5 000 inhabitants, a share similar to settlement patterns in Germany or Italy today. In the states in the southwest (Yoruba country), up to 90% of the population would have lived in localities of more than 5 000 inhabitants. This profile of spatial distribution of the population, ten times greater than countries in the same part of Africa at the same time, appears unrealistic.

The rank-size distribution with a slope of less than -0.4 could reflect a willingness to define subequally sized administrative entities (Figure 4.3). Hence, the Nigerian localities of 1963 correspond to territorial subdivisions consisting of units of which the anglo-saxon classification is *settlement*. The corresponding French translation is "lieu habité" or "établissement humain". The settlement does not have a given surface area. It enables the counting of inhabitants living one place. If its surface is measurable on a map, it will vary as a function of the outlines of the built up area and time.

This idea is confirmed by the high percentage of failed attempts to localise localities. In fact, the name of these districts does not normally correspond to a recognised toponym (place name), town or village, but to a non-delimited area and where the main town does not always correspond to a village's name. In the Niger Delta, three quarters of the toponyms used in the 1963 census cannot be found. In the State of Sokoto, in 1963, only the two biggest localities, Sokoto (89 000 inhabitants) and Gusau (69 300 inhabitants) and perhaps Kaura Namodo and Wurno, included a settlement of more than 10 000 inhabitants. The definition of localities aims increasingly to "preserve" the rural environment rather than define village-type entities, their centre, peripheries and their rural surrounding areas.

It is not unusual that agglomerations are created at the crossroads of different localities, so that the population figures do not correspond to any morphological entity (Figure 4.4). A, B, C and D are names of the administrative localities, but for which today there is no cartography. Inherited from ruralist policies, designed to stabilise rural areas and protect their agricultural production, this configuration of townships is still common in agricultural areas of the American central plains. If the political and administrative aim of the subdivision is to govern rural areas, it is understandable that agglomerations emerge on the edges of administrative entities and not in the centre. Because of their location, these agglomerations organise local trade and offer basic services (schools and clinics). In Nigeria, eight identified agglomerations could not be associated with a name. The most populated had 13 500 inhabitants in 2010. These agglomerations do not exist at the political level and are not found on any map.

In 1952, towns exceeding 5 000 inhabitants were defined as localities; the concept of locality was akin to that of "settlement" in Ghana. In 1963, localities with more than 20 000 inhabitants were considered urban. However, these were not the same sort of administrative entities. The list of urban localities existing in 1963 was published, but the figures were based on the unreliable official results and were not based on any physical concept of urban. The remaining localities with fewer than 20 000 inhabitants seem to be only administrative perimetres around a large village, or just territorial subdivisions arbitrarily combining scattered population settlements for administrative purposes.

In conclusion, not only do the 1991 and 2006 censuses fail to provide urban population figures, but the concept of "town" as from 1963 was ambiguous and the figures were not comparable with the 1952 census. Given these constraints, it is impossible to estimate the population of small agglomerations based on the 1963 census.

Inconsistencies between inventoried population and the physical extent of agglomerations

As seen in the 2008 Africapolis I report, correlating the 1963 census data with the actual expansion of agglomerations illustrates these inconsistencies. Some examples were chosen to highlight the inconsistencies. However, this method of showing inconsistencies based on current observations does not allow for estimating the population of small Nigerian towns for the period 1960 to 1980.

Dukku – Gombe State, LGA of Dukku

In the 1963 census table (Vol. *Northern*), this locality was cited in the *"Native Area District"* (NAD) of Kwami, attached to the *Census District* of Dukku Kwami, located in the *Native Authority* of Gombe, in Bauchi State". It was credited with 29 100 inhabitants, yet after carrying out data corrections (see above) 21 500 inhabitants are estimated. An aerial photo taken in 2002 shows that 40 years later the agglomeration's surface area was not more than 3.5 km², hence approximately 20 000 inhabitants (Plate 4.1). By applying the population growth rate observed in the region, at the beginning of the 1960s Dukku's population would have been 3 000 and not 20 000 (certainly not 30 000). The assumption that the 1963 census figures were inflated does not suffice to account for the magnitude of this discrepancy. The *locality* probably referred to an extended administrative perimetre, including several villages, hamlets and dispersed houses. Unfortunately, the 1963 census cartography cannot be found.

Plate 4.1
Dukku in 2002

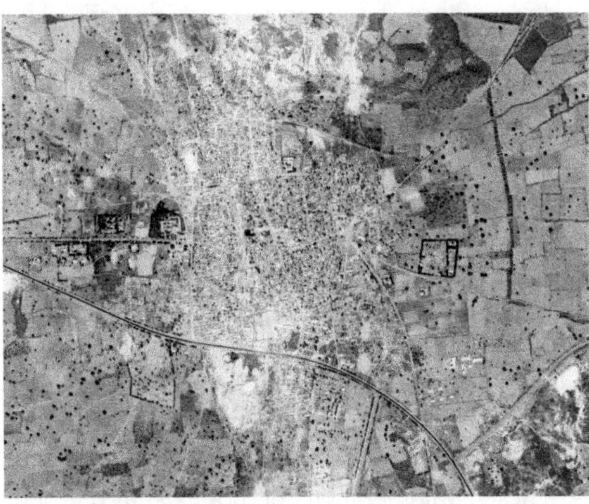

Sources: Google Earth (2012), Dukku, Nigeria, Available at http://www.google.com/earth/download/ge/agree.html (Viewed 29 November 2012)

Song – Adawama State (Gongola State until 1991), LGA of Song

Song is the headquarters of the LGA which, according to the 1963 census, had 8 400 inhabitants, or 5 000 in 1962 after the correction. At this point in time, it was a *locality* of the NAD of Song, in Adamawa *Census District*, of Adamawa *Native Authority*, in Adamawa State. The agglomeration's surface area was 3 km² in 2008 (Plate 4.2). Taking into account the type of housing and the urban density observed in the states of Adamawa and Taraba, there could not have been more than 6 500 inhabitants per km². In 2002, the population was approximately 19 000 inhabitants. This implies that Song's population in 1963 has been over-estimated, but the corrected figures for 1962 could be correct. Again, there is no cartographic document to confirm this hypothesis.

Plate 4.2
Song in 2008

Sources: Google Earth (2012), Song, Nigeria, Available at http://www.google.com/earth/download/ge/agree.html (Viewed 29 November 2012)

Kalgo –Kebbi State, LGA of Kalgo.

In 1963, Kalgo was attached to the Sabon Birni NAD, the *Census District* of Sabon Birni, the *Native Authority* of Sokoto, in Sokoto State (Northern Region). Since, it has become the LGA headquarters of Kebbi State. The agglomeration's surface area was 1.4 km² in 2005, containing approximately 10 000 inhabitants (Plate 4.3). It reportedly had 9 500 inhabitants in 1963, or 7 700 in 1962 after correction. However, our estimates from applying the region's growth rate would rather imply a population of 4 500 in 1963. Kalgo is a good illustration of an agglomeration where there is no ambiguity about its current surface area or its urban dynamics. A detailed observation clearly distinguishes an old centre and more recent extensions (Plate 4.4).

Plate 4.3
Kalgo in 2005

Sources: Google Earth (2012), Kalgo, Nigeria, Available at http://www.google.com/earth/download/ge/agree.html (Viewed 29 November 2012)

Plate 4.4
The former centre of Kalgo (zoom)

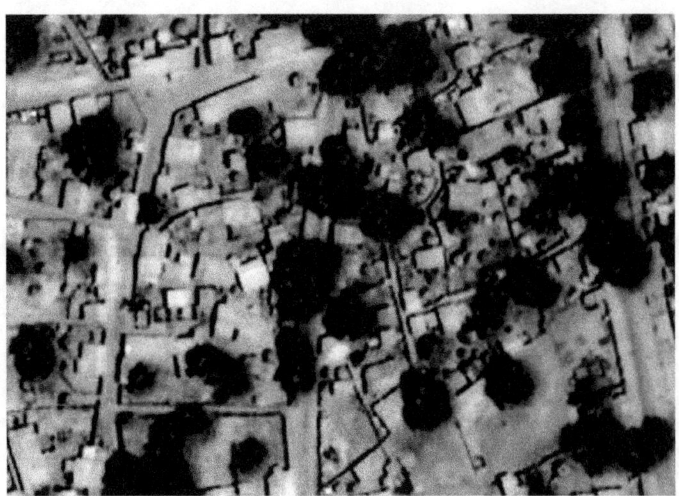

Sources: Google Earth (2012), Kalgo, Nigeria, Available at http://www.google.com/earth/download/ge/agree.html (Viewed 29 November 2012)

Otu –Oyo State, LGA of Itesiwaju

In 1963, Otu was listed in the Western Region and in Oyo State, *Census Division* of Oyo Central and *District* of Iseyin. Today, this agglomeration is the headquarters of the Itesiwaju LGA in Oyo State, having a surface area of 1.5 km² in 2006, with 10 000 inhabitants and a density that is similar to other towns in its region. Yet in 1963 it would already have had 10 400 inhabitants, and 8 300 inhabitants in 1962 after correction. Otu is also credited with 6 500 inhabitants in 1952 census. This either implies a very slow growth rate, or that the 1952 and 1962/63 census figures include much more than the agglomeration (Plate 4.5).

Plate 4.5
Otu, 2006

Sources: Google Earth (2012), Otu, Nigeria, Available at http://www.google.com/earth/download/ge/agree.html (Viewed 29 November 2012)

Accepting the figures of the 1963 census, would mean that in 2006 around 250 towns would have barely more, and some cases much fewer inhabitants, despite fifty years of demographic growth that has seen Nigeria's population triple. While it is always possible that population growth has slowed in some Nigerian towns, population decline and stagnation are uncommon in the region. These are particular cases that are linked to shoreline erosion affecting cities like Banjul (The Gambia) and Keta (Ghana) or to destructions of civil wars like in Sierra Leone and Liberia. Tragic events might have occurred in Nigeria, but they could not explain the negative or almost zero population growth in so many towns, or even the complete disappearance of some *localities* recorded in 1963 census, that today do not appear on any map.

In conclusion, while inconsistencies can certainly be due to the well-known over-estimation of 1963 census figures, they cannot explain the magnitude of the differences between census data and reality, confirmed by the independent morphological identification of official data.

Cities and "locality": A biased population threshold

Logically, the greater the size of the localities the more it fits the concept of a city. In 1963, in localities with over 50 000 inhabitants the population size corresponds to the population of known cities, even if the provided figures included rural areas, similar to the examples of Otu, Kalgo and Song. At what population threshold can it be considered

Map 4.2

Urban sprawl of Lagos and administrative subdivisions in 2010

Source: e-Geopolis – SWAC/OECD 2015

that the population of a locality corresponds to the population of a city? The official 1963 Nigerian definition considered a locality with 20 000 or more inhabitants to be urban. Dukku (21 000 inhabitants) is a good example where the population figure corresponds to a very large territorial constituency, within which the agglomerated big village represents around 15% of the population inventoried. There are no answers to these questions due to insufficient documentation. Consequently, it is almost impossible to establish estimates for urban figures for the years 1960, 1970 and 1980.

Agglomerations made up of several localities: The case of Lagos

Although the aim was to structure a mostly rural environment, the Nigerian administration had to acknowledge, as of the 1960s, the existence of big cities. While in rural areas only a small part of the population of the administrative locality lived in an agglomeration, some agglomerations were already made up of several localities. This was the case of Lagos, with an estimated population, by national and international sources, of 665 300 inhabitants in 1963. However, contrary to previous examples, this figure corresponded to only one administrative entity, the city of Lagos, which at the time already was just one part of the actual agglomeration. Already by 1963 the agglomeration was spilling over to the north into the localities of Mushin (150 100 inhabitants in 1963), Mushin Railway (22 200 inhabitants in 1963), Itire (28 000) and Igbo (7 300), forming an urban agglomeration of 865 600 inhabitants.

Today, the old subdivisions are seriously called into question, with the current agglomeration no longer corresponding to any of the former administrative entities (Map 4.2). Lagos State extends over 3 900 km^2 and is divided into 20 LGAs, of which only two carry the toponym of the former capital, Lagos Mainland and Lagos Island. Strictly speaking, "Lagos city" no longer exists. The agglomeration, covering 863 km^2 in 2010, far from remaining in Lagos State, is very much spilling into Ogun State to the north.

A consequence of the statistical "overlooking" of Lagos' outskirts in 1963 is a continuous overestimation of Lagos' population growth over the past 50 years. Interestingly, Lagos is one of the rare cases where the 1963 census results seem right. In the November 1991 census the agglomeration's population was set at 5.15 million inhabitants and at 9.25 million in the March 2006 census (10.59 million in 2010 according to the e-Geopolis definition). Based on a population of 665 300 inhabitants in 1963 (census), instead of 865 600 (including the population of the bordering localities), the average annual growth rate between 1963 and 1991 is 7.6% rather than 6.6%. At such

Plate 4.6
Case where a LGA borderline should follow a water body

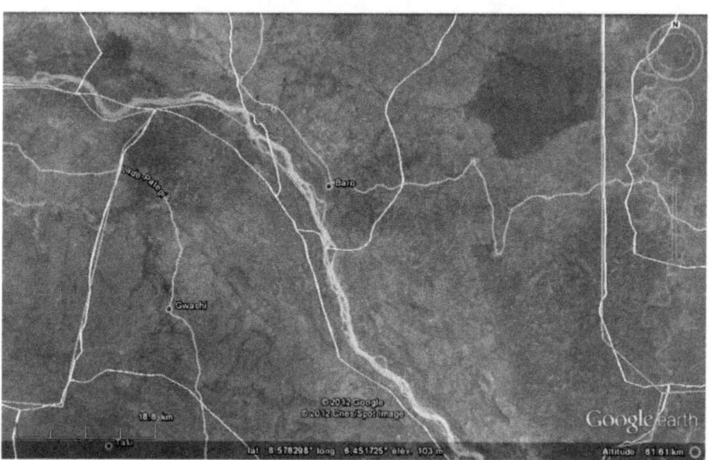

The LGA border in this example from the central area of Nigeria should run along the Niger River bed. Yet the discrepancy is up to 5 kilometres on the ground. However, to the right of the image, the LGA borderlines coincide closely with those of the State (here the southwest corner of Federal Capital Territory).

Sources: Google Earth (2012), Abuja, Nigeria, Available at http://www.google.com/earth/download/ge/agree.html (Viewed 29 November 2012)

a rate and over a 28-year period, the difference is considerable. Yet, as Lagos represents the archetype of over-populated large cities in large developing countries, such biased figures are often provided as an illustrative example in literature on urban growth in these countries. Still marginal in 1963, the expansion of agglomerations beyond the official administrative limits becomes widespread with urban sprawl, the infill of rural areas of the Niger Delta (continuous densification) and linearisation of agglomerations along the infrastructure networks. These three forms of urban growth will be developed later.

4.4 A DEFICIENT ADMINISTRATIVE CARTOGRAPHY

Imprecise mapping of LGA boundaries

Only one publicly available digitised dataset of the borderlines of the 774 LGAs exists[3]. Superimposed on a map, it presents challenges for estimating urban populations. The LGA boundaries correspond well to international borders and the shoreline. The discrepancies observed are essentially the result of the varying levels of resolution between images (high resolution) and the delimitation of borders (lower resolution). For example, this is the case in lagoon regions where coastlines are imprecise due to mangroves and variations on intertidal zone surfaces between low and high tides. However, the outlines of the LGAs correspond less closely to the Nigerian states' borders from which the authors put together the base map. In addition, the precision of map details becomes very poor within the same "state".

In Plate 4.6, a satellite image taken from Google Earth is overlaid with the LGA map published by the *Independent National Electoral Commission* (INCEC), "Nigeria, Atlas of Electoral Constituencies". The borderlines of the LGAs are outlined in white and that of the states in dark grey, the main roads are traced in thicker yellow and water bodies are blue.

Outlines impossible to correct

There are other errors that are impossible to correct cartographically. They appeared in 2012 during the systematic alignment of a locality to an LGA. It should be kept in mind that in 2006 there was no official registry of localities. How can one therefore proceed in determining each agglomeration's hierarchical affiliation to an LGA? Two alternative sources were used: primary schools and post offices registries. Both sources have an address attributed which contains the name of

Plate 4.7

Outlines of cities: The case of Gombe

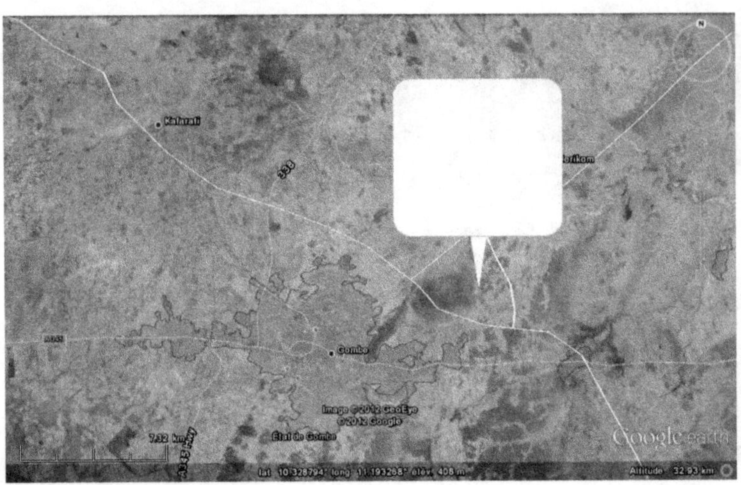

Sources: Google Earth (2012), Gombe, Nigeria,
Available at http://www.google.com/earth/download/ge/agree.html (Viewed 29 November 2012)

The LGA of Gombe (outline shown by the bubble) is compared to the city's actual location. On the ground the city is located much further to the west and neither its shape nor its expansion corresponds to that of the LGA. Contrary to the previous example, in this case it is impossible to correct the LGA's borderlines. It is possible that the surface area of the Gombe LGA is too small; and it could equally be that it is a conurbation. In this case, the borderlines would certainly not be in the right place, but the shape would be correct. The agglomeration having grown strongly, it simply spilled over the border of the LGA.

Plate 4.8

Outline of big cities and inexactness of the outline: The case of Idah

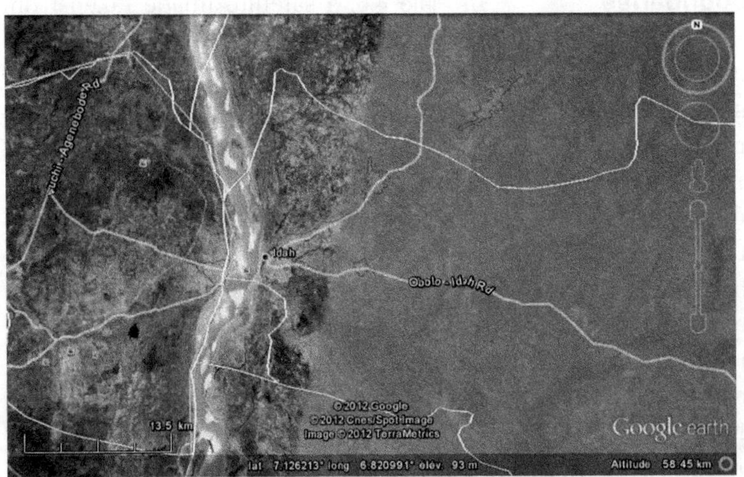

As in the previous case, the shape of the urban LGA Idah does not fit over the agglomeration. Also, the border should be on the riverbed. The expansion of the LGA does not correspond to that of the agglomeration, but the LGA is much bigger than the agglomeration.

Sources: Google Earth (2012), Idah, Nigeria, Available at http://www.google.com/earth/download/ge/agree.html (Viewed 29 November 2012)

the LGA to which it belongs. Yet, on a map some of them appear located in a neighbouring LGA, confirming the impreciseness of borderlines on the LGA base maps.

Similarly, big cities are divided into several LGAs, of which some, on the periphery, include large areas of the surrounding countryside. The administrative unit of LGA does not allow for a

Plate 4.9

Outlines of big cities: The case of Maiduguri

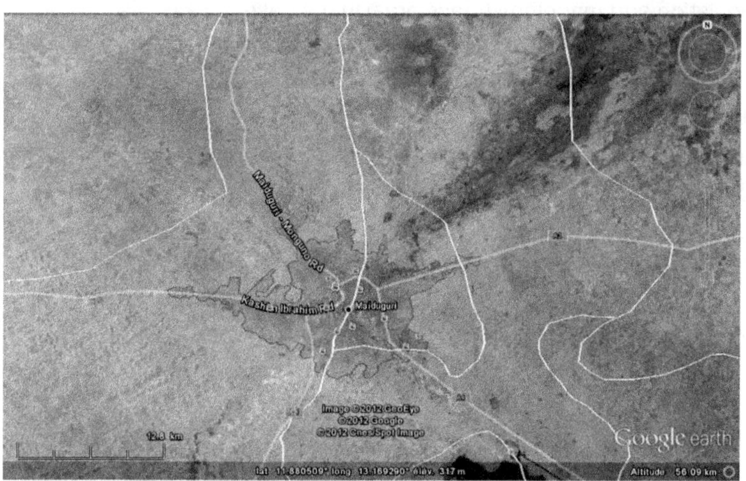

Sources: Google Earth (2012), Maiduguri, Nigeria,
Available at http://www.google.com/earth/download/ge/agree.html (Viewed 29 November 2012)

As in the preceding two examples, the shape of the LGA does not correspond to that of the agglomeration of Maiduguri. In any case, its territory would be too small to contain the entire urban area. It is obvious that the Maiduguri LGA (137 km²) is much smaller than the actual agglomeration (153 km²), which naturally implies an expansion across the LGA's borders. This example helps understand that some agglomerations in the database can be more populated than their LGA eponym.

precise estimate of an agglomeration's population. Or, as is the case in Lagos, where the perimetre of the LGA does not cover the entire agglomeration and the population of the neighbouring administrative entity has to be added.

Correcting inconsistencies in LGA figures

The estimated population of agglomerations in 2010 is based on a recent chart by the Nigerian National Bureau of Statistics (NBS), published in 2012. The chart shows the population by LGA according to the 1991 and 2006 censuses, and provides an estimate for October 2011. This document was particularly helpful in identifying inconsistencies among the various demographic sources. In addition, the dataset of LGAs published by *Independent National Electoral Commission* had inverted some of the LGAs, causing errors in the Africapolis 2008 estimates. Correcting these errors (Lagos State, in particular), as well as cartographic improvements, explains some of the size of the changes between the two versions. Without providing an exhaustive list, two examples are:

- There is a difference of 5 million inhabitants between the total population summed by State and the total population summed by LGAs;
- Box 4.1 provides more details on the corrections carried out by the authors.

Box 4.1
Main errors found in the 2011 population chart by LGA

1. Inversion of statistical data (population and mapping/surface area) in the case of:

- Illela and Gada (Sokoto State): This error existed in the original publication of 2006 census figures, and was corrected in subsequent publications;
- Amuwo Odofin and Apapa (Lagos): Data inversed in the original version;
- Doguwa and Nassarawa (Kano): Idem. In addition, 245 000 inhabitants are missing in Nassaraw, original version;
- Kaura and Kauru (Kaduna): Seems to come from an error of alphabetical ordering in the original version.
- Girei and Gombi (Adamawa): Idem.

2. Significant differences of population sizes in the two 2006 series:

- LGA of Uvwie: 189 000 inhabitants compared with 101 000 in the initial version.
- LGA of Bassa (Plateau): 189 000 inhabitants compared to 139 000 in the preliminary versions.
- Abi (Cross River): 114 000 compared with 144 000 inhabitants
- Ifelodun and Irepodun (Osun): Figures in the original versions were much higher. The correct series seems to provide fewer inhabitants:

Ifelodun	206 042	96 444
Irepodun	148 610	119 590

- Nassarawa (Kano): See above.
- Obi (Benue): 99 000 compared with 149 000. This figure does not seem coherent with the 1991 data because it shows a decline in the population.

2011 estimates

The total population of Nigeria summed by population figures by state is five million inhabitants less than the total population summed by LGAs. For Lagos State alone the difference is 3.56 million. The Alimosho LGA (Lagos) is credited with 3.56 million inhabitants in 2011 compared with 1.3 million in 2006, an implied annual growth rate of 22% and a density of 20 000 inhabitants/km^2 which seems unjustifiable given single storey dominated housing structure and the important presence of industrial buildings in Ikotun.

4.5 METHODOLOGY

The statistical situation in Nigeria remains problematic. The lack of local data is a major constraint to estimating urban populations by agglomeration. At this point, only a geographic approach can help detect certain shortfalls, errors or gaps in demographic data. A geographic approach tries to answer the question, "Where are the cities and what size are they?". This approach allows for a verification of the existence, or lack thereof, of a settlement independent of official sources. The cross-referencing of satellite images and aerial photographs, field visits and actual land use characteristics provide objective methods of verification. However, this verification method can be subject to certain biases, such as:

- lack of images corresponding to the date of demographic sources;
- lack of high-resolution images (heavy cloud cover or image resolution above 50 metres);
- lack of information on the occupancy of settlement areas;
- errors and/or doubts concerning the "correct" toponym hindering the identification of an agglomeration.

The proposed approach to estimating agglomerations' population takes into account:

- local settlement characteristics, based on the systematic mapping of identified agglomerations' location and their physical imprint;
- theoretical models that classically characterise settlement systems.

Identifying agglomerations and estimating their population

Agglomerations with a surface area greater than 1 km^2 are systematically identified and all LGA headquarters no matter their size. It turned out, however, that some LGA headquarters are only a collection of administrative buildings forming an agglomeration of a few hundred inhabitants.

The physical imprint of 1880 agglomerations (less than 700 in 2008), with a continuously built-up area with space between buildings not exceeding 200 metres, have been digitalised and placed in a map. Most of the satellite images used are from Google Earth, of which 95% are high resolution (as opposed to 50% in the 2008). Maps 4.3 and 4.4 are the result of this preparatory work.

Once it has been assigned its administrative position, each agglomeration is entered into the e-Geopolis database with a 7 digit code: "state" (2 digits), LGA (2 digits), eponym "locality" (3 digits) to which a country code is added "NGA" (Table 4.4). When an agglomeration spans several LGAs, or even several states, the name and code of the eponym locality are used.

The population of each agglomeration is then estimated at the end of 2006. The population in 1991 and the corrected population in 2011 is then calculated by applying the population growth rate of the agglomeration's LGA (or LGAs). For LGAs that did not exist prior to 1991, the 1952 and 1963 census data are recorded. In the case of small agglomerations, these data are not very comparable with those post-1990. Therefore, the database only contains data that seem probable after applying the above described corrections and verifications.

Taking into account settlement structures

Three types of local morphologies – grouped, linear and scattered – have been identified in order to estimate agglomerated population based on density. The surface area of agglomerations in each environment is compared with that of agglomerations in neighbouring countries such as Niger, Benin, Cameroon and Chad, for which there is more precise population statistics and geographic information.

Map 4.3

Physical imprint of agglomerations greater than 1 km², southern Nigeria

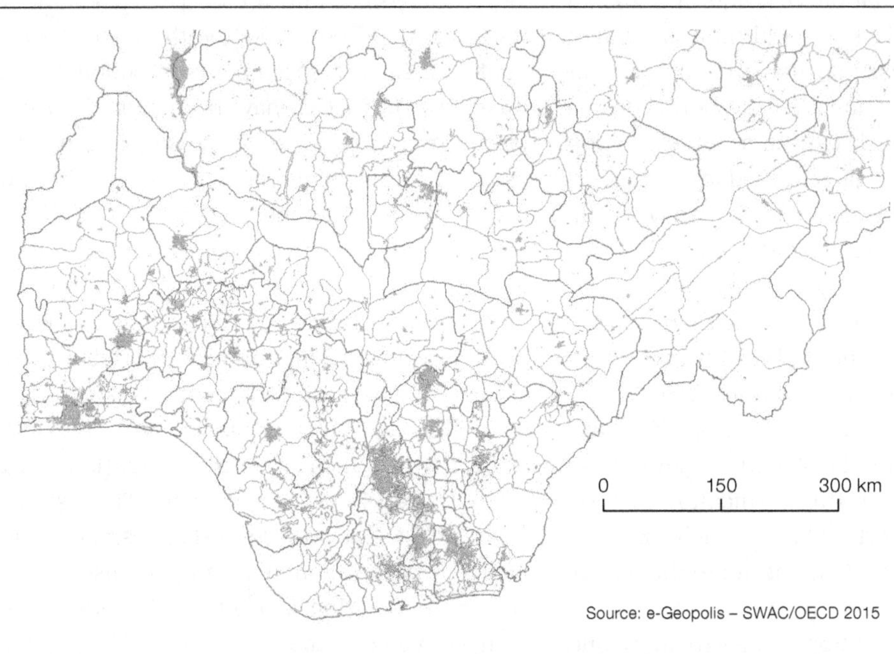

Source: e-Geopolis – SWAC/OECD 2015

Map 4.4

Physical imprint of agglomerations greater than 1 km², northern Nigeria

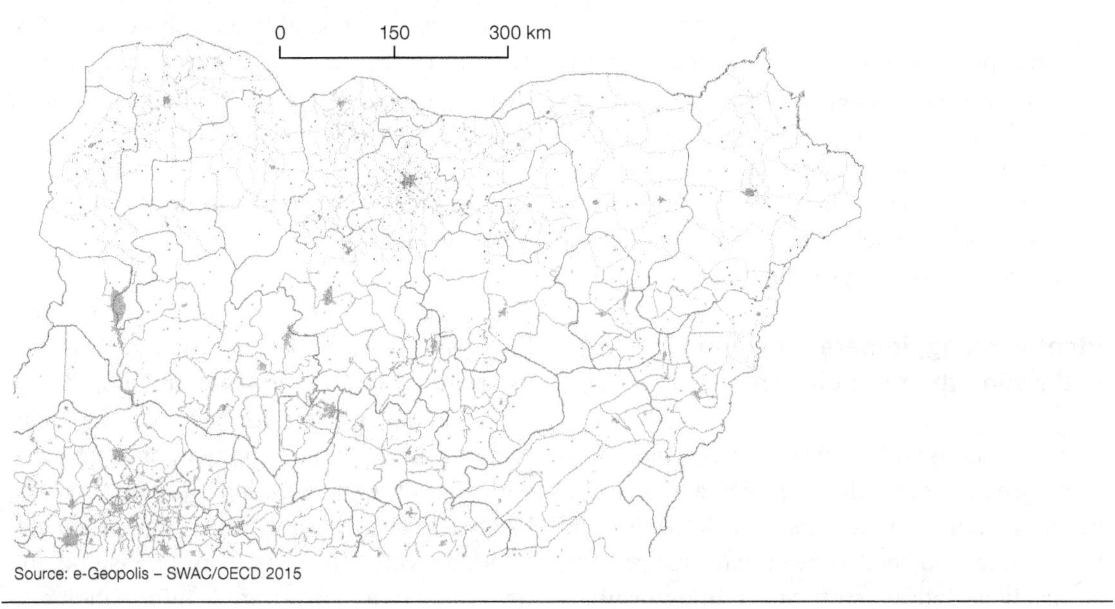

Source: e-Geopolis – SWAC/OECD 2015

Table 4.4

Example of coding: Orogun agglomeration, Delta State, Nigeria

State	Code	LGA	Code	Locality	Code	e-Geopolis code
Delta	11	Ndokowa West	1112	Orogun	1112002	NGA1112002

Grouped settlements

In general, this is the most common type of settlement in the Sahelian and Sudanian zones, the flatter parts of the country's northern region, except for areas close to the Cameroon border. The shape of villages is usually square or circular. Traditionally, buildings are very compact, road networks are very narrow and empty spaces are rare. The density of a built up area in big villages and small cities can often reach 1 000 homes per km^2.

This type of grouped housing is defined by a succession of big villages with no particular hierarchy and located in agricultural zones with no other settlements. The population density of big villages is between 6 000 and 8 000 inhabitants/km^2. According to our estimates, only Alkamu has over 10 000 inhabitants (Map 4.5). However, very high demographic growth automatically leads to the reclassification of existing big villages as they cross this threshold. Eventually, this process will result in a massive increase in the number of small agglomerations, leading to a higher level of urbanisation without necessarily implying rural migration.

Plate 4.10
Grouped settlement in Alkamu (Sokoto State), 10 300 inhabitants end 2006

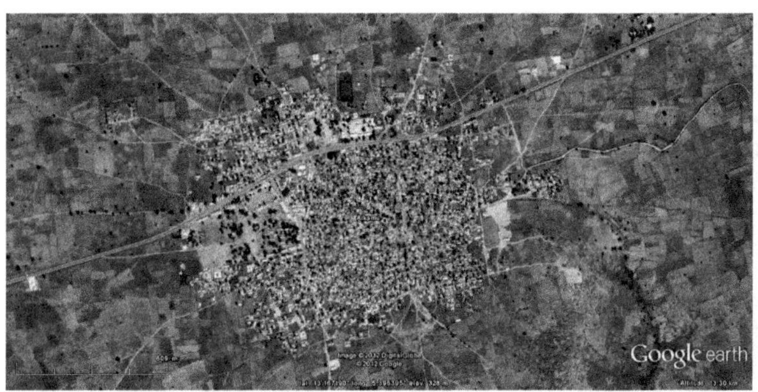

Sources: Google Earth (2012), Alkamu, Nigeria, Available at http://www.google.com/earth/download/ge/agree.html (Viewed 29 November 2012)

Map 4.5
Location of Alkamu

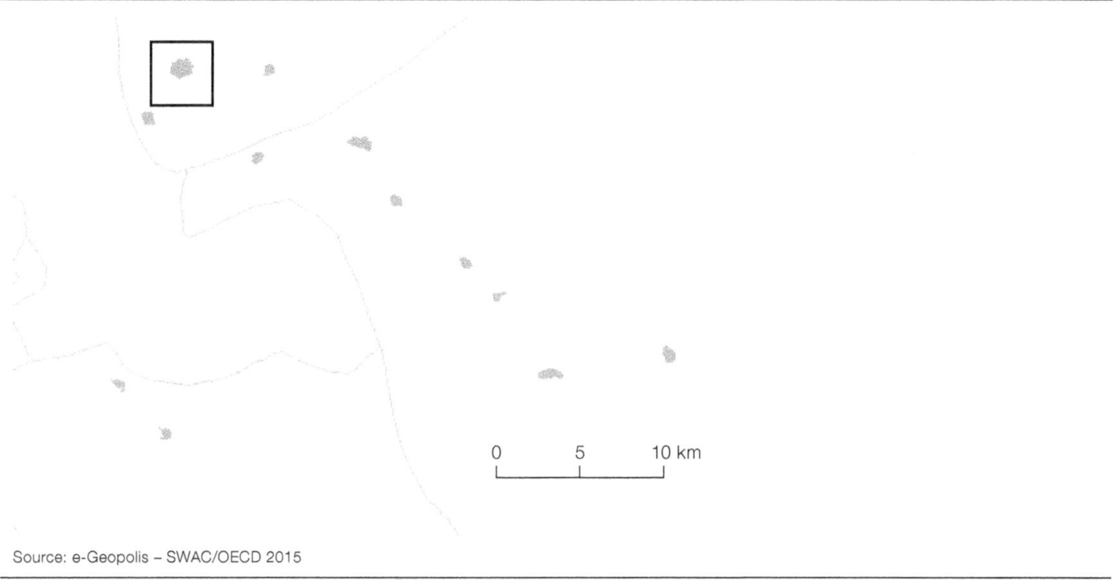

Source: e-Geopolis – SWAC/OECD 2015

Linear settlements

Traditionally linear settlements are characteristic of the forest regions in the south as well as hilly areas in the east. Since 2000, they are more widespread along routes throughout almost all of the country, except for in the north where land use seems better managed.

Plate 4.11 illustrates how intensive post-1990 urbanisation along the route led to the merging of the Uromi and Irrua agglomerations forming one agglomeration of 120 000 in 2006. In 2010, the density of the built up area reached between 5 000 and 6 000 inhabitants/km², slightly lower than grouped settlements. This process of linearisation produces merging between various large, initially distinct, villages, which keep their identity and their name. This process leads to an increase in the size of agglomerations, but does not affect the level of urbanisation if the merged agglomerations were already urban prior to merging.

Plate 4.11
Detail of the Uromi/Irrua agglomeration (Edo State) in 2006

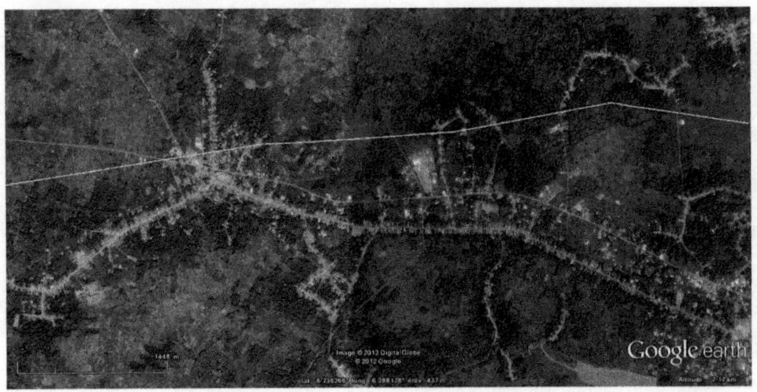

Sources: Google Earth (2012), Uromi/Irrua, Nigeria, Available at http://www.google.com/earth/download/ge/agree.html (Viewed 29 November 2012)

Map 4.6
Location of Uromi/Irru

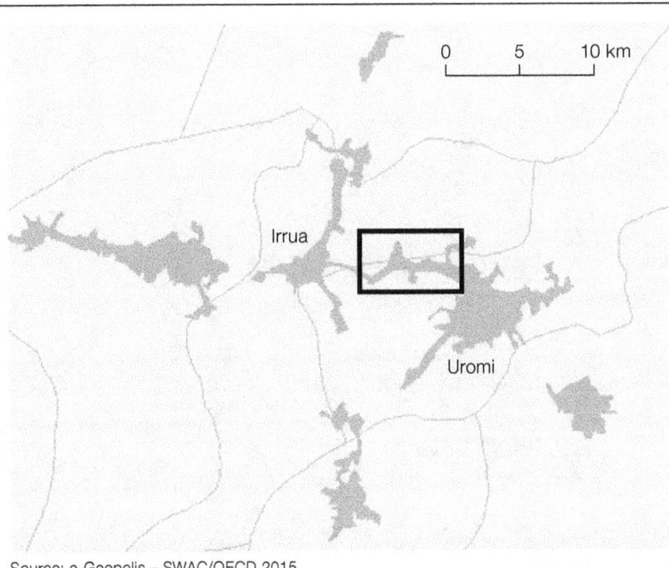

Source: e-Geopolis – SWAC/OECD 2015

Scattered settlements

Most scattered settlements in Nigeria are found upstream of the Niger Delta in the states of Anambra, Imo, Abia, Ebonyi and Kogi. They can also be found all over the country (Jos plateau, on the piedmonts in the east).

Plate 4.12 illustrates a spectacular example of scattered settlement in Nigeria. This type of settlement can also be found in other regions of the world such as in the West Kenya, Zoulou countries, South Africa and in Brittany, France, etc. Settlements in other delta regions, however, can be densely grouped (Egypt).

In this region of Nigeria, settlement is traditionally rural and very spread out with few cities. Under the effect of strong population growth, the rural infill changed the landscape into vast, sparsely populated agglomerations with a density of 2000 to 3000 inhabitants per km², already above rural densities. The hyper-rural environment quickly becomes meta-urban once the demographic density threshold has been reached. While in 2010 the word "urban" can certainly still seem excessive in characterising these zones, that will be less and less the case in the future. By 2030 densities will have increased by 50%.

Plate 4.12

Supposed "rural" sector south of Onitsha

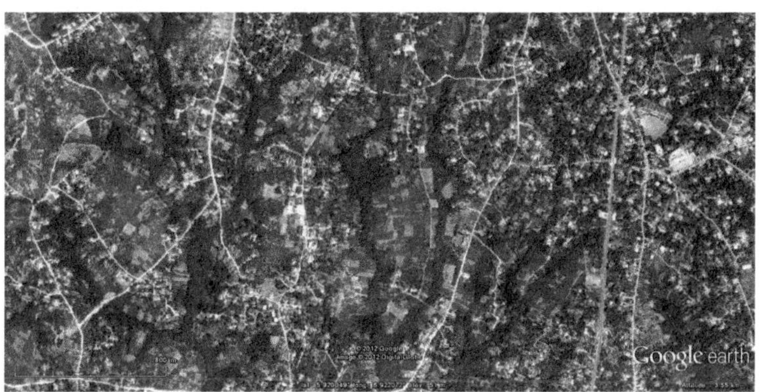

Sources: Google Earth (2012), Onitsha, Nigeria, Available at http://www.google.com/earth/download/ge/agree.html (Viewed 29 November 2012)

Map 4.7

Location of the southern sector of Onitsha

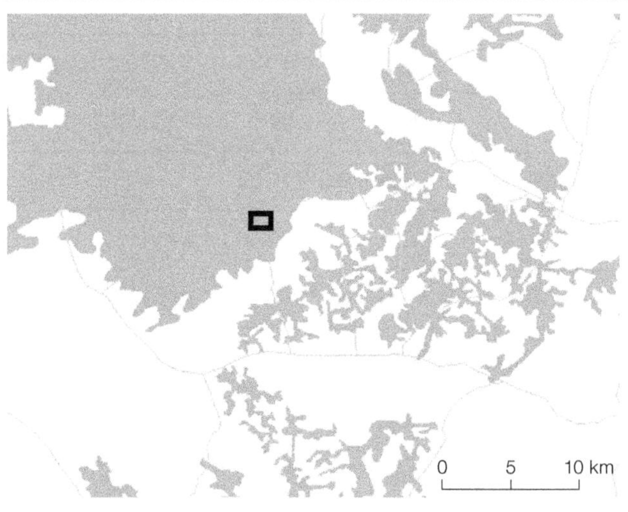

Source: e-Geopolis – SWAC/OECD 2015

4.6 RESULTS

To estimate the agglomerated population in 2010, data for three different years are used: Nigeria National Bureau of Statistics data that provide the population by LGA in the 1991 and 2006 censuses, (see above[4]). The population estimates of the preceding periods were based on the 1963 census (Vol. 6), 1962 pre-census and the censuses from 1952 (Vol. 4), 1931, 1911 (without the Northern Protectorate), 1901 (idem) and 1891 (idem).

Level of urbanisation and total population

Table 4.5 provides the main results at national level. In 2010, the total population of the 1 020 agglomerations of more than 10 000 inhabitants was 76.4 million. The total surface area covered by these agglomerations is less than 14 000 km², in other words 46% of the population was living on 1.5% of the national territory.

The level of urbanisation of a territory, also called rate of urbanisation, depends as much on the estimate of the total population as on the urban population. The method developed by e-Geopolis to estimate the agglomerated population is however not applicable to the rural environment, and hence the total population. Nigeria's total population estimates are based on existing demographic sources and the adjustments explained earlier.

The urbanisation rate of 46% in 2010 is high compared to West African average and even Africa in general. This result confirms the assumptions highlighted in the introduction:

- Urbanisation in Nigeria is ancient and started much earlier than in other countries in the region. Nigeria has two big regions at the origin of ancient urbanisation processes. In addition, there are genuine industrial clusters and, although still insufficient, a developed network of communication infrastructure. Furthermore, due to its geographic position, Nigeria has the qualities of a transition area between the Sahel and West Africa, with low levels of urbanisation, and forested Central Africa, with the highest level of urbanisation in Africa

Table 4.5
Nigeria and West Africa

	1950	1960	1970	1980	1990	2000	2010
Total population (millions)							
Nigeria	31.8	39.2	49.3	65.7	87.0	119.4	166.2
West Africa	30.2	38.2	50.4	67.8	88.6	114.0	156.4
Number of agglomerations							
Nigeria	99	209	310	480	584	792	1020
West Africa	53	96	183	290	420	625	927
Urban population (millions)							
Nigeria	3.6	8.4	12.4	20.2	32.7	48.4	76.4
West Africa	1.7	3.6	7.7	14.5	23.7	36.1	56.4
Level of urbanisation (%)							
Nigeria	11.4	21.4	25.2	30.8	37.6	40.6	46.0
West Africa	5.7	9.4	15.4	21.4	26.8	31.7	36.0

Source: e-Geopolis – SWAC/OECD 2015

(Congo, Gabon, Cameroon). As a result of these characteristics and its population size, Nigeria accounts for 51% of the West African population, but 58% of its urban population. This share is in constant decline because the rest of West Africa, starting at lower levels of urbanisation, is urbanising more quickly. In 1950, more than two thirds (68%) of the West African urban population lived in Nigeria.

- The size and influence of Lagos, which rapidly became the biggest agglomeration of Sub-Saharan Africa. With 10.6 million inhabitants in 2010, the agglomeration is home to 6% of the country's total population, which is very low compared with other West African countries but still sizeable given Nigeria's demographic size. In fact, the population of Abuja, the new capital, increased 10-fold in 20 years (1.1 million in 2010) on account of direct and indirect employment linked to the government. Abuja could grow to 2.8 million inhabitants in 2020 by absorbing surrounding towns. Lagos is still by far the biggest agglomeration in West Africa. The Onitsha conurbation, the second biggest agglomeration Nigeria, is also second in the region.
- Above all however, is the impact of the huge conurbations that have formed since 2000 due to the densification of scattered settlements in the highly populated regions of the Niger Delta. These emerging conurbations, with lower densities of inhabitants per km², add five to seven percentage points to the national level of urbanisation given the high share of the Niger Delta regions in the total population. The population density east of the Niger Delta, Imo and Anambra States and in some LGAs of the neighbouring states of Aba, Rivers, Akwa and Ibom, reached 1 000 inhabitants per km² in 2010. In 1990 Onitsha was an agglomeration of 620 000 inhabitants. By absorbing 20 agglomerations that already had more than 10 000 inhabitants in 1990, it grew to an agglomeration of 6.3 million inhabitants in 2010. Far less dense than Lagos, it covers over 1 925 km². Uyo (1.9 million inhabitants), Nsukka (1.5 million) and Aba (1 million) are similar examples. The more classic agglomerations like Kano (3.1 million inhabitants), Ibadan (2.5 million), Port Harcourt (1.4 million), Benin City (1.1 million) and Kaduna (990 000 inhabitants) are still very dense.

While this study does not eliminate all data inconsistencies, we can however, predict that by 2050 all of the central and northern part of the Delta will form one contiguous urbanisation. Regions that three quarters of a century ago were exclusively rural will be entirely urbanised following a relatively extensive model. With continuing population growth, density will increase; new constructions will continue to densify the landscape. High-yield intensive farming is still possible within "extensive" conurbations. This has been observed in the Flanders region of Belgium, the Holland region of the Netherlands, the west of Kenya, the Nile Delta and Al Jazirah in Sudan, Japan, Java, the Philippines and Taiwan. This activity is a lot less commonplace, indeed impossible, in the highly populated agglomerations in other Nigerian regions.

The identification of agglomerations based on a unique set of rigorous statistical criteria shed light on the existing diversity of agglomerations (types and forms). These differences are essential for understanding the overall dynamics of "Nigeria's urbanisation", which differs greatly from region to region.

Distribution: Results in accordance with Zipf's law

In 2010, Nigeria had one agglomeration with more than 10 million inhabitants, 10 agglomerations with more than one million inhabitants, 90 of more than 100 000 and 1 020 of more than 10 000 inhabitants. The number of agglomerations increases approximately 10-fold when dividing the sample's minimum urban threshold by ten. The distribution of agglomeration in Nigeria results in a balance remarkably consistent with the model of K. Davis and with the rank-size law of G.K. Zipf (Davis, 1970). This underscores the quality of the database obtained by applying the e-Geopolis method.

The good fit of the rank-size distribution (R2 = 0.998) correlates to the vastness of the urban system as well as to the diversity of the country's environments and resources. A context of liberalism and urban development gave free rein to a "natural" form, consistent with a Pareto distribution of large numbers.

A slope slightly less than 1 indicates significant pressure from small agglomerations. Smaller in size and more homogeneous, the population of these agglomerations is much easier to estimate. However, estimating the size of medium to large cities by applying this method will depend more on official demographic data. As this data is suspected of being inflated, one could have expected the population of big cities to be over-estimated, which is not the case. This further supports the reliability of the study's estimates.

Figure 4.5
Rank-size distribution of agglomerations in Nigeria

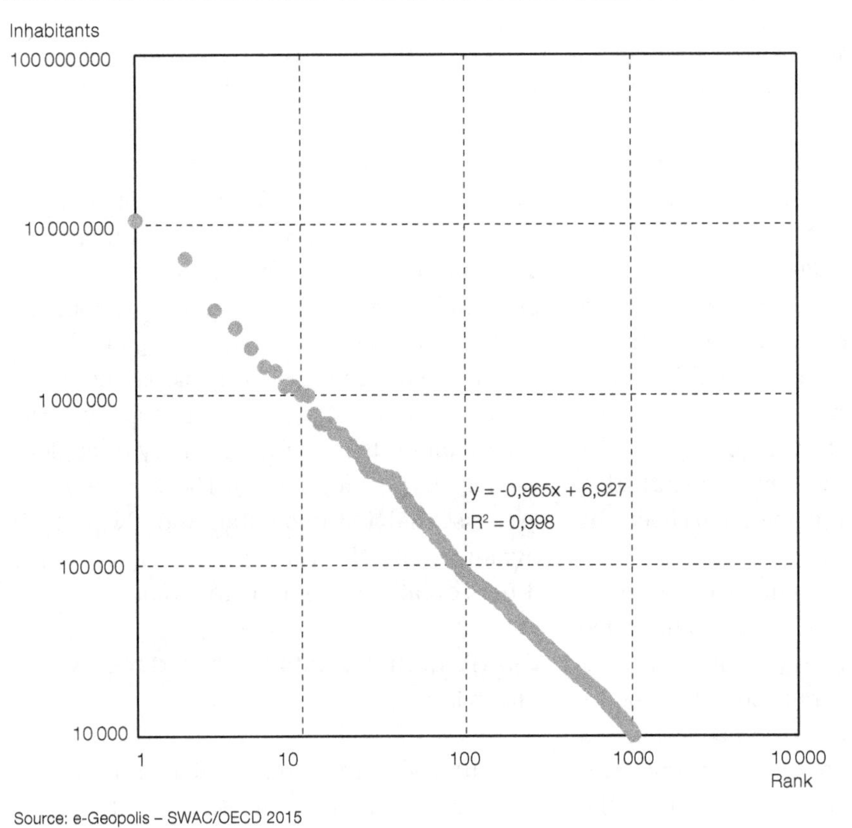

Source: e-Geopolis – SWAC/OECD 2015

Table 4.6
Distribution of urban agglomerations by size in 2010

	Number	Surface area (km²)	Population	Share in total urban population (%)	Density (inhabitants/km²)
10 million or more inhabitants	1	863	10 590 000	14	12 270
1 000 000 to 9 999 999 inhabitants	9	5 110	19 870 000	26	3 890
100 000 to 999 999 inhabitants	80	4 081	21 549 000	28	5 280
10 000 to 99 999 inhabitants	930	3 917	24 412 000	32	6 230

Source: e-Geopolis – SWAC/OECD 2015

Does density increase with agglomeration size?

Density can be linked to land values in big cities. Consequences are smaller housing units, taller buildings and intensified land use. In Nigeria, where vertical expansion of housing is limited, density is expressed by the intensity of land use. This intensity compensates for the presence of non-residential buildings and zones (administrations, monuments, facilities, industrial zones) (Plate 4.13).

Generally linear, the relation between size and density shows a high degree of variation depending on environment, especially in a country as large and diverse as Nigeria. In addition, diversity of the urban tissue of big cities has to be taken into account: grouped and dense in the centre and in residential working class neighbourhoods, while linear and/or dispersed along the edges. At the same time, several agglomerations have modern neighbourhoods where collective housing projects dominate. Towns of all sizes can include industrial zones of varying importance (Plate 4.14), military camps, university campuses, and land reserves in the form of forests or large enclaves, even vacant land within the agglomeration.

Plate 4.13

Working class neighbourhood in Kaduna: Single storey structures, narrow road network, high population density and continuous land cover

Sources: Google Earth (2012), Kaduna, Nigeria, Available at http://www.google.com/earth/download/ge/agree.html (Viewed 29 November 2012)

Plate 4.14

Industrial zone, Kano: Surface area 21 km^2

Sources: Google Earth (2012), Kano, Nigeria, Available at http://www.google.com/earth/download/ge/agree.html (Viewed 29 November 2012)

4.7 CONCLUSIONS ON NIGERIAN RESULTS

Despite their shortcomings, the results can be considered the most reliable on the population of Nigerian cities and towns and on the identification of an exhaustive list of agglomerations[5]. While there are probably very few omissions in the listing of agglomerations, there can be significant bias with regard to population estimates. Individual over- or underestimations of 20% to 30% cannot be excluded. Population numbers of agglomerations between 50 000 and 250 000 inhabitants are the most difficult to estimate and the most problematic region is the Niger Delta. The population size of the biggest agglomerations is reliable, assuming that the figures of the 1991 and 2006 censuses are also reliable. However, the population estimates of small towns are the most reliable and present the main added value of this work.

A more significant increase in the number of small towns than anticipated

Already one of the main results of the 2008 study, the number of small agglomerations is greater than anticipated. Nigeria is following the same trend as many countries in the South with strong population growth. The improved database has made this trend even more apparent (through improved image quality, as well as by the systematic analysis of the country's 774 LGAs).

A re-evaluation of the emergence of big conurbations in the Delta.

In the Niger Delta region, the densest part of the country, the physical expansion of agglomerations is much greater than what was thought in 2008. The landscape of the southeast of the country evolved much quicker than was previously estimated. These results disrupt the national hierarchy of the country's agglomerations, while, contrary to the preceding paragraph, many small agglomerations are lost as they are merged into larger agglomerations.

The results also raise new issues such as the generalised infill in the Niger Delta, an excessive linearisation of urbanisation of certain regions, and the disorganised proliferation of small, dense urban centres still considered rural. The impact of these emerging issues on future development processes will need to be measured and analysed.

NOTES

1 *These tests indicate a satisfactory quality of the data.*

2 *As a result of the sharing of German Kamerun in 1920, the Northern Cameroons was formed by two disjointed areas located on the north and south of the border putting Cameroon (French) and Nigeria (English) in contact. It was administered and recensed with Northern Nigeria, without officially belonging to it.*

3 *Independent National Electoral Commission (INCEC), "Nigeria, Atlas of electoral constituencies", Garki, Abuja, Nigeria. This background can be downloaded from: www.mapmaker.com.*

4 *Directly obtained from the NBS, this document seems not to have been published.*

5 *Due to no other information source.*

Bibliography

Bairoch, P. (1985), *De Jéricho à Mexico. Villes et économie dans l'histoire*, Collection Arcades, No. 4, Gallimard, Paris.

Davis, K. (1970), "World urbanization 1950–1970", *Population Monograph Studies*, No.4, 9, Institute of International Studies, University of California, Berkeley.

Mustapha, A. R. (2006), "Ethnic Structure, Inequality and Governance of the Public Sector in Nigeria", *Democracy, Governance and Human Rights Programme Paper*, No. 24, United Nations Research Institute for Social Development, Geneva.

ORGANISATION FOR ECONOMIC CO-OPERATION AND DEVELOPMENT

The OECD is a unique forum where governments work together to address the economic, social and environmental challenges of globalisation. The OECD is also at the forefront of efforts to understand and to help governments respond to new developments and concerns, such as corporate governance, the information economy and the challenges of an ageing population. The Organisation provides a setting where governments can compare policy experiences, seek answers to common problems, identify good practice and work to co-ordinate domestic and international policies.

The OECD member countries are: Australia, Austria, Belgium, Canada, Chile, the Czech Republic, Denmark, Estonia, Finland, France, Germany, Greece, Hungary, Iceland, Ireland, Israel, Italy, Japan, Korea, Luxembourg, Mexico, the Netherlands, New Zealand, Norway, Poland, Portugal, the Slovak Republic, Slovenia, Spain, Sweden, Switzerland, Turkey, the United Kingdom and the United States. The European Union takes part in the work of the OECD.

OECD Publishing disseminates widely the results of the Organisation's statistics gathering and research on economic, social and environmental issues, as well as the conventions, guidelines and standards agreed by its members.

OECD PUBLISHING, 2, rue André-Pascal, 75775 PARIS CEDEX 16
(44 2016 01 1 P) ISBN 978-92-64-25222-6 – 2016

www.ingramcontent.com/pod-product-compliance
Lightning Source LLC
LaVergne TN
LVHW081418110826
845149LV00010B/1791